May You Never Stop Dancing

May You Never Stop Dancing

A Professor's Letters to His Daughter

John D. Lawry

Saint Mary's Press
Christian Brothers Publications
Winona, Minnesota

For Lili,
my daughter, former soldier in *The Nutcracker;*
and Ruth,
my mother, who taught me to dance.

Genuine recycled paper with 10% post-consumer waste.
Printed with soy-based ink.

The publishing team included Michael Wilt, development editor; Laurie A. Berg, copy editor; Lynn Dahdal, production editor and typesetter; Maurine R. Twait, art director and cover designer; cover and title page photo, Roy Gumpel, Tony Stone Images; author photo, Paul and Diane Sattler; pre-press, printing, and binding by the graphics division of Saint Mary's Press.

The acknowledgments continue on page 127.

Printed in the United States of America

Printing: 9 8 7 6 5 4 3 2 1

Year: 2006 05 04 03 02 01 00 99 98

ISBN 0-88489-535-1

Contents

Preface to the New Edition

Dear Student,

Ten years ago I wrote this book of letters to my daughter, Lili, who was then a freshman in college. Little did I know at the time that it would have such a profound effect on many other young people. I know now because of the many letters (and more recently e-mail!) that I have since received from both young people like yourself and from parents.

When the original publisher, Sheed and Ward, decided in 1996 not to reprint the book, I assumed that would be the end of a very satisfying and longer-than-average (eight years) life of a book. However, as the letters and e-mail continued from readers expressing their appreciation, I began to realize that the ideas contained in the book were still speaking to the next generation of high school and college students after my daughter's college class of 1989. When Saint Mary's Press expressed an interest in bringing out a new edition, I was very enthusiastic.

What you have in your hands is the new edition. I have tried to update it as much as possible without losing any of the charm of the original edition. It has not been an easy task. The revision has taken the form of several new letters as well as minor changes in the original letters.

Many students who have read the book become very curious about my daughter. Suffice it to say that Lili graduated on time in 1989, majoring in finance and entrepreneurial studies. Two years later she married the young man referred to in the letter "Too Steady Too Soon—Relationships." Lili is presently finishing her MBA, and last year she started her own business as a food broker in the Boston area.

In closing I want to repeat my request for feedback, because I love to receive letters from readers. I wish you every success in your first year of college. Indeed, may you grow in wisdom as well as knowledge, and may you never stop dancing!

Blessings,
John D. Lawry
Lawry@mmc.marymt.edu

P.S. I want to thank my colleague, Milt Steinberg, for saving me tons of time with his computer wizardry.

Preface to the 1988 Edition

Dear Student,

I got the idea of writing this book several years ago when my daughter was still in high school. I wanted to pass on to her all the academic wisdom I had accumulated over the twenty years I had been in the business of teaching undergraduates. Since my degree is in educational psychology, I have learned a lot about the learning process in the classroom, and I wanted to share all the discoveries I have made with my daughter, and now with you. As a result much of this book is of a very practical nature: writing term papers, enrolling in the "right" courses, getting A's, beating test anxiety, and passing statistics ("sadistics"). Believe it or not, these are things that no one is likely to tell you, and as a result, most students have to learn them on their own. I know I did.

I also write about things you might expect: the importance of writing, reading poetry, keeping a journal, and falling in love with the library. But I don't stop there. I have come to realize that what goes on outside the classroom frequently determines what goes on in the classroom. So I write about getting along with your roommate, taking good care of yourself, handling stress, being honest in relationship, and making friends with your "shadow."

Finally, I see what Mother Teresa called spiritual deprivation in so many young people today. And so I write about developing your inner self, meditation, finding God in nature, and the power of forgiveness. I hope you will keep an open mind when you read these letters in particular, because they are the ones that make this book unique. In fact, they are the ones that will keep you dancing, a metaphor for living life to its fullest. In both meanings of the word, it is only recently that I have really begun to dance, and I write so that you will not wait as long as I did.

I have taught psychology to young men and women for the past twenty-two years at five colleges and universities, both in the United States and in the Far East. My daughter, Lili, is presently a college junior, and her name appears in the salutation of the majority of the letters. Indeed, Lili has taught me more about your generation than all the textbooks I have read on adolescent psychology. Occasionally, names have been changed to protect confidentiality, and I have taken some poetic license with references to actual events, but they are based on a deep sense of reality.

I want to thank my daughter for being my best friend and critic, because I know she always tells me the truth even when it is not easy to hear. And I want to thank my fiancée, Elaine Zablotny, for her unfailing love and support while I toiled with the manuscript. I also want to thank the thousands of students to whom I have taught psychology over the years and who have taught me how to be a better teacher. I want to acknowledge my colleagues at Marymount College, Tarrytown, and the other institutions where I have taught, for their expert advice, their friendship, and their encouragement to write this book. Finally, I want to thank the Sister Servants of Mary Immaculate at Saint Mary's Villa in Sloatsburg, New York, for taking care of me during my three-month sabbatical retreat while I finished the manuscript. I am especially indebted to Sister Jonathan for her spiritual direction and sisterly friendship.

In closing, I hope you will find what you are looking for, and any suggestions for this book's improvement in future editions will be greatly appreciated. I wish you every success in your first year of college; may you grow in wisdom as well as knowledge, and may you never stop dancing!

Blessings,

John D. Lawry
Marymount College
Tarrytown, New York 10591

"College Life Is Great"

Dear Lili,

Thanks for your letter the other day with all the information and the good news, "College life is great!" I sincerely hope it remains so for the next four years.

Now that you are living away from home for the first time without an adult supervisor, I hope you will use this opportunity to become the kind of person you want to be. Having gone through the arduous maze of college selection and succeeded in being accepted at the college you wanted most (next to Georgetown!), I have a few bits of advice to share with you as a result of being a college professor for some twenty years now.

The idea I would like to expand upon in this letter is that a college education should not be thought of exclusively as what goes on in the classroom. I see my students growing by what transpires in the dormitory, the cafeteria, the athletic field, and the local pub as much as in the classroom—if not more so. For this reason I am pleased you chose to live away at school. Students who live at home and commute do not get the same education.

At the age of eighteen, you are still very much an adolescent and are struggling with the tasks of adolescence, namely self-definition, identity, social interaction with peers, and eventually mate selection, not to mention the more academic cultivation of an intellectual life and career choice. (Please note the order of the last two items!) It is very important that you be somewhat on your own now in your struggle to become your own person, but also that you remember that your mother and I are only a phone call away. You are not alone out there.

Jean Piaget, the great Swiss psychologist, once said that the ideal grammar school is one in which the students spend half the day with

11

the teacher and the other half with one another in the absence of the teacher! That ratio, I feel, is just about right for college as well. That is why it is so important to choose a college because of the students you will learn from and with as well as the faculty you will learn from and with. An old teacher of mine used to say that the best colleges are best because they attract the best students. In other words, think of your fellow students as teachers, and you will multiply the number of faculty available on your campus by a factor of ten or more.

While on the subject of teachers, I would like to make the point that ultimately you are your own teacher, or at least that is what you should be aspiring to become. By the time you graduate, the best teacher you could learn from should be yourself. What I mean is that you should be concentrating primarily on the skills that you will need in order to facilitate the learning that you will have to do for the rest of your life (lifelong learning). So I am pleased that you have chosen a college that places so much emphasis on the liberal arts, even for a business major, because the liberal arts are designed to help you become your own teacher, not only with regard to lifetime learning skills but also to making the best use of your leisure time as well. Now is the time to discover and become friends with the world's great writers, artists, and composers so that you will not be restricted to television for entertainment for the rest of your life!

I hope all of this doesn't sound too professorial, but I feel I have a few things to say to you as a result of being "in the business" for these past twenty years. Let me know what you think.

Take care, Sweetheart, and know that I miss you and love you.

Love,
Dad

P.S. Don't forget to take your vitamins.

From High School to College: Making the Transition

Dear Lili,

I was just reading the alumni newsletter of one of my alma maters (Duquesne University), and it reported on a new course for freshmen entitled "New Student Seminar." It talked about how freshmen frequently make the mistake of thinking college will be like high school and therefore have a lot of difficulty making the necessary adjustments.

One of the biggest adjustments that students have is learning to make new friends away from home. When freshmen arrive on campus, it appears that everyone knows everyone else. Very often a freshman will conclude that "everybody has friends but me." That's not true, of course, but that's how it appears. Thus, one of the biggest problems for freshmen is loneliness.

Unfortunately, freshmen find a number of ways to cope with initial loneliness that are less than healthy. One strategy is to keep the old support group (family and friends from home, for example), enabling the student to avoid the necessity of extending herself and finding new friends. These are the students who rarely join any campus activities or clubs and can't wait to get home for the weekend.

Another strategy is to find one other lonely person (same sex or opposite sex) and form what is called a symbiotic relationship. They become a couple and are always together, not realizing that the primary motivation is fear. In other words the relationship is ingrown and precludes any connection with outsiders.

Perhaps the worst strategy is to indulge behaviors and attitudes that are signs of depression: poor eating and sleeping habits (either too much or too little), insufficient exercise, loss of self-esteem, poor performance in classes, and even thoughts of dropping out, or worse, suicide. This student is a prime candidate for the counseling center and needs all the help she can get.

It is for this reason, more than any other, that colleges spend so much time and money on the freshmen orientation program. I know it sometimes feels like a waste of time and a drag, but it has a very good rationale behind it. So, begin the orientation with an open mind and with the goal of meeting as many people as possible. From these initial contacts eventually will emerge many of the friends you will make among your classmates during the year.

Attitude is very important during these first days and weeks. If you adopt a superior, preppy, private-school snobbishness, you will discover that it doesn't work. Remember that college is a whole new ball game, and all the players as well as the rules have changed. What worked in high school may backfire in college. One good piece of advice is to be humble. You may be bright, but you still have a lot to learn about college. Nothing is worse than a freshman who thinks she knows it all. So, don't feel obligated to impress everyone; just be yourself—your best self! Do that and you will be well launched to a wonderful first and critical year in college.

Sorry, I have to run to class now. Take care, and enjoy these first days of the college experience. See the challenges rather than the opportunities to complain, and let me know how it is going.

Love,
Dad

Getting the "Right" Courses

Dear Lili,

We have just finished course registration for freshmen, and it reminded me of some tips I wanted to give you. As a student adviser, I always tell my advisees to choose courses, especially electives, by the professors who teach them as much as, if not more than, by the subject. I feel that students should be exposed to the best minds the college has to offer, the relevance to their major notwithstanding. Remember that a college education is supposed to help you learn the skills that you will need in your future career, and this is usually taken care of by the requirements in your major. Beyond that, a "higher" education is supposed to introduce you to the much-maligned liberal arts, and that's the part of your education that distinguishes college from a training institute. Think of it as a final opportunity to be exposed to the great literature, music, drama, and art of the world in such a way that you will spend a significant part of the rest of your life cultivating and refining your tastes. A college education should prepare you as much for your future leisure time as it is does for your life's work.

Choose teachers who love their subjects and who love their students. Nothing can be more exciting than the classrooms of such teachers. Both loves are important in a college teacher, for as Goethe said, the teachers who had the greatest influence on his life were not the most brilliant but were those who loved him. How do you find these teachers? Just ask a few seniors who the best teachers are. The ones who come to virtually everyone's lips without thinking are the ones I'm talking about. These teachers might be "hard," but years from now they are the ones you will remember most fondly because they challenged you and taught you the excitement of creative thinking. May your campus be blessed with at least a few great teachers!

Gotta run to class now!

Love,
Dad

Remembering People's Names

Dear Lili,

We did something very interesting in class today. I introduced an exercise designed to help the class get to know one another's names. It is a simple exercise whereby the first person in a circle introduces herself by saying her first name and then the name of someone else she would like to be just for a day (living or dead, real or imaginary, male or female). I chose Boris Becker because of my fondness for tennis. The second person begins with the name and then the "alter ego" of the first person: for example, "Dr. Lawry would like to be Boris Becker." Then she says her name and who she would like to be. The third person follows suit, and it continues until the last person goes around the room saying everyone's name, followed by their alter ego.

With a class of twenty students, a number of people expressed the fear that they couldn't remember all those names. What was interesting was the fact that the people who had the greatest difficulty remembering were the ones who had announced that they couldn't do it. What I wonder is whether they had created a self-fulfilling prophecy, somehow contributing to the fulfillment of their own negative prophecy. My suspicion is that such thinking and the expression of it act as a kind of negative programming that operates through the unconscious. The unconscious is always listening and cannot discriminate between positive and negative suggestions. If so, it seems to me that we should be able to transform the negative to positive and use the dynamic to our advantage rather than as a way of undermining ourselves. The moral, of course, is that if you want to remember people's names:

- Tell yourself that you *will* remember everyone's name, not that you'll be unable to.

- Stay relaxed while you are being introduced.
- Make some connection between the person's name and something else (anything, it doesn't matter!).

The technique really works, and I only ask that you give it a fair test. Let me know what happens!

Must run for now.

Love,
Dad

What No One Ever Told Them About College (A Survey)

Dear Lili,

I conducted a survey recently in my general psychology class of twenty-four students, mostly freshmen. I asked them to "list five things that you wish someone had told you about college before coming to Marymount, things that you had to learn on your own." I thought you might be interested in the results. The responses are ranked in order of frequency of occurrence (the number in parentheses represents the number of students who gave that answer; those without a number had one response each) and are stated in summary form or, in some cases, verbatim.

1. Importance of self-discipline (time management, and so on) (9)
2. Money problems (8)
3. Roommate problems—"Don't expect her to be your best friend!" (6)
4. Amount of responsibility (independence) placed on students (5)
5. Amount of work and time required for studying (4)
6. Heterogeneity of student body (moral standards, social class, and so on) (4)
7. Missing Mom's home cooking (3)
8. Diversity of teaching quality (3)
9. Difficulty attached to registration and course selection (3)
10. Great opportunity for growing up (3)
11. Missing family and friends (3)
12. Learning to get along with so many people (2)
13. Too much walking! (2)
14. I love it! (2)
15. Don't be afraid to get involved. (2)
16. People care more than I anticipated.

17. The amount of cheating
18. Assertiveness works
19. Importance of library skills
20. Getting a husband seems to be more important than getting an education.
21. Students are here because of Daddy.
22. No surprises!
23. Need for a car at a residential college
24. What to bring!
25. Importance of attending class
26. Importance of note-taking skills
27. Scary not knowing where I am going
28. Immaturity of other students
29. Time flies!
30. What to do after college?
31. Don't get sick!
32. Be yourself!
33. Too many requirements!
34. Poor social life
35. The food is good!
36. Not enough washing machines
37. Not enough heat!
38. Not enough hot water for showers!
39. Courses are more interesting than high school.
40. Get yourself known by faculty and administrators; they are human too!
41. Difficulty of being a commuter at a residential college
42. Teachers are so nice and helpful.
43. Theft in the laundry room

So there you have it, Lil. Let me know what you think and what you can identify with. To self-discipline!

Love,
Dad

Teaching from the Heart

Dear Lili,

Several years ago a student came to my office for some help with statistics. It was a bad day, and I found myself becoming annoyed at her apparent ignorance of elementary operations—procedures I felt she should have learned in high school. Finally, I was no longer able to contain my irritation, and I blurted out the accusation that she should already know the material. At that moment she looked at me, and in a tone of pure objectivity, said, "Dr. Lawry, I really don't think your remark is very helpful."

My eyes met hers, and for a moment I was speechless. Her candor and maturity, not to mention courage, pierced my heart. After a long breath, I was able to apologize, and we went on with a successful tutorial. When the student departed, I realized that the experience taught me a valuable lesson, one that I would like to share with you.

The longer I teach, the more I come to the realization that what we call teaching is but creating an environment in which the student learns or, perhaps more accurately, teaches himself or herself. This environment has many components, but the most important one, I am convinced, is love. As I mentioned in a previous letter, the German Romantic poet and dramatist Goethe said that the teachers who had the most influence on him were not the most brilliant but were those who loved him. After twenty years of college teaching, I am finally beginning to understand what Goethe meant.

Few authorities in my field of educational psychology have written about the place of love in the classroom, exceptions being the late Carl Rogers, and Leo Buscaglia. In a little-known study published in 1974, two researchers (David Asby and Flora Roebuck) found that what Carl Rogers calls empathy, congruence, and positive regard, as measurable characteristics in grade-school teachers, contribute significantly to classroom learning.

In other words, teachers who measure high in empathy, congruence, and positive regard produce students who score higher on standardized achievement tests than teachers who measure low. Not only that, but teachers high in empathy have better student attendance rates and fewer students with school phobia. Unfortunately, this is an isolated study on a topic that needs further research and understanding.

A number of years ago for Christmas, my sister Barbara gave me a copy of Buscaglia's book *Living, Loving and Learning.* In it Buscaglia laments that all too frequently parents neglect to tell their children that they love them. The next time I saw you at boarding school in your junior year, I asked you whether you could remember the last time that I had told you I loved you. You thought for a moment and said, "Gee, Dad, it must be a long time ago, because I can't remember." Needless to say, I told you that I loved you as I dropped you off, and I felt especially close to you as we hugged good-bye. For some reason I haven't had any trouble telling you that I love you ever since.

The point I am trying to make is that I haven't yet learned to tell my students that I love them, but on my office door now hangs the title page of a book of poetry by Swami Muktananda that reads, "I Welcome You All with Love." I wish I had the courage to say that on the first day of class. May you find at least one teacher who loves you!

I love you,
Dad

Becoming Your Own Teacher

Dear Lili,

I was thinking about the idea of becoming your own teacher and the fact that everyone must take responsibility for their own learning. Unfortunately, our school system reinforces passivity, as a visit to almost any classroom at any rung of the educational ladder (except perhaps kindergarten!) will amply demonstrate. Who is doing most of the talking, lecturing, thinking? The teacher. Who is doing the sitting, listening, note taking? The student.

The more I teach, the more I see that the typical college classroom is not a very efficient place to learn anything. It pains me to hear college graduates say, "I think I will take a course in such and such." By the time you graduate, taking a course should be unnecessary. To learn something on your own would be a test of whether you really have become your own teacher. (For example, I have taught myself to use the computer by writing these letters to you.)

Taking responsibility for your own learning means not blaming the teacher if you don't learn anything (which may or may not be reflected in the grade!). Try to see the teacher as a guide or a facilitator, one who presumably knows more about a particular subject than you do, a model to be imitated perhaps, a participating learner. If you need the teacher to be a motivator as well, you are in trouble, because your learning will be contingent upon the teacher being able to motivate you. If you feel that he or she is boring, uninspiring, dogmatic, or whatever, you will not learn, and you will have given responsibility for your own learning over to someone else.

How do you know if you have learned something? The classic psychology textbook definition says that learning is a relatively permanent change in behavior that is brought about by *experience* (in other words, it is not induced by things like drugs, fatigue, illness, and so on). So if last week you couldn't ride a bicycle and today you can, you are then able to say that this change in behavior must be due to your having "learned" to ride a bike. (This is what is called an inference, because you can't see the learning but infer its existence to explain the change in behavior.) Therefore, everything that you learn should have some effect on your behavior. (I am using the word *behavior* to include psychological phenomena such as perception—smelling a rose, and cognition—solving a problem, as well as motor behavior—riding a bicycle.)

It follows then that what does not produce change in you somehow isn't learned. If you read a book and it doesn't change you in some way, then you haven't really learned anything from reading it. You might argue that you chose not to change because you disagreed with the author—a kind of negative learning. That's legitimate; but in all other cases, if you haven't changed, you haven't learned. The next time you read a book, concentrate on the changes it might introduce into your life; otherwise you have wasted your time! (Though I must confess that the changes may not be immediately apparent and, for much of what you learn in college, probably won't be.) What I am arguing for is a vigilance for connecting what you are learning to your life, for making it relevant. That's fairly easy to do in my discipline of psychology, but it should be the goal of everything you learn, from art and architecture to Zen and zoology.

Taking responsibility for your own learning also means cultivating efficient study habits. All too often I hear students respond to a poor grade on an exam with, "But I stayed up all night studying for it." A good learner never stays up all night studying for an exam. By doing so the student puts himself or herself at a disadvantage by taking the exam after a sleepless night, and also reveals that he or she has left everything until the last minute. To coin a proverb, Procrastination is the mother of failure.

The one characteristic that seems to identify good students in my experience is that they have learned to anticipate the teacher. This strategy of staying ahead of the teacher gives the student a tremendous advantage. The lectures become much more meaningful because the student has already read the material and now has a context in which to listen to the lecture. The listening becomes much more productive; indeed, it becomes *active* listening. Furthermore, the learning becomes distributed over a period of time rather than massed at the end, when the students have real critical limits operating and a radical diminishing of returns after a few hours of cramming. Another way of thinking about this is that the good student has simply learned to organize his or her time better. One of the things that you should be learning in college is how to use your time so that you get the work done and still have some time left for play and fun.

A corollary of this, of course, is that you should never waste time. *Waste* here is a tricky word. One person's "wasted" time is another person's leisure. One of the things you discover as you get older is that time is one of life's most precious gifts. I suppose balance is the key here. An old Latin adage says, *age quod agis!*—Do what you are doing!—or perhaps less literally, Be here now!

Keep in mind also that you (or someone else, like your parents) are paying a lot of money for the privilege of sitting in that classroom; therefore, only a very good reason should justify cutting a class. All too frequently I see students hurting themselves by not attending class and by not even bothering to find out what happened while they were absent. Try to arrange your schedule so that you can attend all your classes, and if for some good reason you must be absent, be sure to find out what happened from a classmate. (Don't bother the teacher, because she or he usually doesn't relish giving the lecture over again. It is your responsibility to find out what was said.) Remember, you are responsible for learning the material that was covered in the class from which you were absent. I find it frustrating when a student attempts to excuse herself from knowing something because she was absent from that particular class.

Absenteeism brings up the whole question of health and taking care of yourself. I see a lot of students abusing their bodies and becoming ill when they should be at the peak of their health. The problem, I think, is that many students have not internalized the good health habits imposed by their parents, and when they are away at school, no one imposes the habits anymore. As a result, students fall into bad habits with regard to sleeping, eating, drinking, and so on. I suppose it is part of the task of discovering one's limits, and many students, it seems, have to discover their limits the hard way.

A final point I would like to make about health is that being a student is primarily a sedentary occupation, and thus it is mandatory that you reserve a certain amount of time each week for exercise. A twenty-minute segment seems to be the minimal period for optimal aerobic effect. A number of studies have shown that students who exercise regularly do better in their studies, probably because it improves their powers of concentration. Centuries ago an ancient Roman writer said that a sound mind in a sound body is the key to a good life. Promise me that when you are finished reading this letter, you will go for a nice walk and think about becoming your own teacher, okay?

Take good care,
Dad

Getting Along with Your Roommate

Dear Lili,

You write that you are not getting along with your roommate. Don't panic. Instead, look upon this as an opportunity to grow. Before you run to the Dean of Students' office in search of a new "roomie," see if you can resolve your differences with the one you have. Try to talk to her and find out what you do that bothers her, and tell her what bothers you. She simply may not be aware. Where you have real differences, such as music versus quiet time, try to work toward a compromise. This is what negotiation is all about, and it is excellent practice for when you are older and presumably married. If your differences cannot be worked out, perhaps a third party, a kind of arbitrator, can help you resolve them. Don't be afraid to ask for help before you ask for a new roommate! On the other hand, don't be afraid to ask for a new roommate if all else fails.

Give it your best shot, and let me know what happens. Good luck!

Love,
Dad

P.S. If you want some perspective on roommates, I strongly recommend reading John Updike's insightful short story "The Christian Roommate." It is a tragicomic account of the tears and joys of two "incompatible" roommates who have much to teach each other and who apparently become lifelong friends. As you know, I believe people come into our life for reasons, either to teach us something or to learn something from us—usually both.

Falling in Love with the Library

Dear Lili,

Before you graduate I hope you discover that the library is one of the most important academic resources available to you on a college campus. Think of every writer of every book in your library as a prospective teacher. In my opinion much of a college education is or should be learning how to use the library. In a sense the local public library will be your "college" for the rest of your life after graduation. The library is your connection with the greatest thinkers who have ever lived, and so it is very important that you learn how to use it.

Implied in all that I am saying, of course, is a love of books, and so I am dismayed at how infrequently college students use the library and how dependent they are upon the librarian when they do. If your college offers a course in using the library, I would recommend it, because the benefits will last a lifetime. If the college does not offer such a course, then perhaps you can get a job there. I learned more about the library by working there than anything I could have learned by taking a course!

When you use the library, don't feel that you must always begin with the card catalog (or, more likely, computer database). Sometimes you will make wonderful discoveries right on the shelves by browsing in the section you are interested in. The library is a great teacher and one that is user-friendly!

Speaking of books brings up the weighty topic of reading. The reading habits you establish now will probably last you a lifetime, so it is a good idea to establish strong habits now. In addition to the assigned reading you are doing for your courses, get into the habit of reading at least one daily newspaper, one weekly newsmagazine, a monthly journal of opinion, and a book a week of your own choosing. Impossible, you say! Once you get into the habit, you will discover that it is not only possible but rather effortless, like eating three meals a day. The truth is that you will never have more leisure time in your life than you do right now, so this is the best time to develop good reading habits.

When I was in college, I always carried a book with me no matter where I went; it was my student badge, and it saved precious time from being wasted. What to read, you ask? I am inclined to answer with the words of Henry David Thoreau: "Read not the Times. Read the Eternities." The best place to begin is the Great Books program, a copy of which is found in Mortimer Adler's *How to Read a Book.* Adler's book itself, by the way, is not a bad place to begin, for it is the best attempt I know of to teach one to read. Interestingly enough, the subtitle of the first edition is, *The Art of Getting a Liberal Education.* The whole curriculum of Saint John's College in Annapolis, Maryland, is built around the Great Books. One of the real handicaps many students face today is not knowing how to read at college level. Apparently not many people know how to teach this basic skill either. Adler, I feel, is an exception, and fortunately he has written down his techniques for all to learn them (assuming one can read them!).

Well, Dear Heart, I'm off to class. Good reading.

Love,
Dad

The Magic of Writing

Dear Lili,

I can't write about reading without in the next letter writing about writing. If students today have poor reading skills, then their writing skills are even worse. This isn't just my opinion or the opinion of writing teachers. Jean-Jacques Servan-Schreiber, the French technology expert and writer, was asked by *Time* magazine to give his opinion of the ways in which Americans excel. Listen to what he said:

> From my first days in the U.S., I have been a regular student and admirer of America. But today the U.S. faces a crisis in education. The level of primary and secondary education is well below the worldwide average. Young Americans entering college can hardly write a decent one-page text. They take little time and no pleasure in reading.

Reading and writing are mutually interdependent skills; good reading should help your writing, and vice versa. I'm sure you have heard it before, but let me repeat, the only way you learn to write is to write. I probably learned to write in college by carrying on an extensive correspondence with friends back home. I was fortunate in having a few friends who knew how to write letters and liked to do so. (I spent my college days in the seminary, as you know—and we were not permitted to use the phone.) The best suggestion I can offer in this regard is to keep a journal and to write in it every day. I require journal keeping in most of the courses I teach, and I am never disappointed in how it seems to help students overcome their anxieties about writing. So get yourself a blank journal and become a writer!

Love,
Dad

Developing the Inner Self

Dear Lili,

In speaking of journal keeping the other day, I was reminded of one of its fringe benefits, which is that it helps you to get in touch with your inner self in a way that no other technique I know of does. A psychologist by the name of Ira Progoff has refined journal keeping into an elaborate and powerful growth system called *At a Journal Workshop*. (It is a book title as well as a workshop, and I recommend that you take the workshop if you have the opportunity.) My favorite description of a journal is from Tolbert McCarroll's *Exploring the Inner World*. Listen to what McCarroll has to say:

> You are on a voyage of self-exploration. You need [a journal,] a log to record the adventure. The journal is not a place for explaining, for asking or answering why. It is not a diary. It is a log.
>
> On this quest the activities recorded are dreams, fantasy art experiences, and similar events. The items are recorded in a simple manner with no comment, editing, or analysis. The journal is a record of what is; not what should be.
>
> There are many other kinds of logs. The master on a ship decides what data to collect, what events to record in the ship's log. . . .
>
> Obtain a good sized notebook. Artists' sketchbooks are inexpensive and ideal in every way. There is usually an embarrassing moment as you look at your new journal. How do you start? We feel the first entry should be very impressive. Do not use the journal to impress yourself, and certainly not posterity. If nothing else works to break the mystique, rip out the first page. The journal is an existential joke book. It is a place to play, to be free and spontaneous. The journal is you—all of you, including the parts that are not introduced into polite society; the immature you, the dreamer, the child. The journal is the place where they all come

together without invitation and without rejection. And you own whatever is there.

There is a haiku by Issa that belongs in the front of every journal:

> He who appears
> before you now
> is the Toad of this Thicket.

Whatever comes, it's my thicket. . . .

My journal is many things to me; above all, it is a companion. It helps me gain self-discipline and keeps my experiences alive.

Discipline is important in this quest. Inner messages are not given to the casual dilettante. Am I really trying to hear myself? This is the basic question. A glance through your journal will tell you whether you are only talking about self-exploration or are actually engaged in the process.

Many of the experiences logged in a journal have a short life span. By your writing them down, their duration is prolonged a few precious moments. The act of recording also allows you to regain some of your emotional involvement each time you return to what you have written.

Each experience is a piece in a puzzle. You could try to work a jigsaw puzzle by using one piece and trying to deduce what the entire puzzle looks like, but it would waste considerable time in unproductive speculation. A better use of your energy and a clearer sense of the picture can be obtained by collecting as many pieces as possible. Each new piece gives additional meaning to the ones already collected. The journal is the table upon which to store and play with the pieces collected. . . .

The disciplines of growth are demanding. Its rewards are not always immediate. Why do it? That is a difficult question. If a person is not committed to his own growth, there is no reason to undertake this journey. If you are committed, then you explore your inner world simply because it is a necessary part of you.

It is not always easy to be ourselves. The first step is really to hear what is going on with us. The masks we wear for the benefit of others often deceive us as well. It is important that we learn to be ourselves. We do this by stopping the attempt to be somebody else. There is a wise biblical proverb:

"Drink the water of thy own well." [Proverbs 5:15]

You must drink your own water, be it bitter or sweet. You must be yourself. If you want to change or grow, you have to accept where you are and be who you are.

The wisdom for growth is within us. Once we have learned really to listen to ourselves we can hear suggestions for our next step. Sometimes there is pain. The wild storms of winter are a necessary preliminary for spring's beauty. Just as bodily discomfort can tell us when we have broken nature's rhythm, the pain in the heart can be a beacon showing us the next step on our journey.

It is through the discipline of keeping a journal that I learn to become me. Without this inner journey I feel incomplete and lonely. I am conscious of all the "oughts" and "shoulds" of life. This is not enough. I want to hear from that part of me that never changes and feel those parts that change every second. It feels good to be me and the more me I am the less conscious I am of me.

Each of us is a necessary part of a long story. It would have been nice if we had been taught our place in the story when we were young children, but a while back it seems as if everyone forgot the story. So we all grew up wondering about our value and our worth. We search for a place where we can belong. Now when we are older and it is harder, we must learn that our value is in being who we are and that we belong here. It is through my journal that I can begin to hear my own story and to search for my part in the story of life.

While on the subject of inner growth, I want to share with you the joys of meditation. I started meditation only a few months ago, but I wish I had started at your age. Somehow the word *meditation* was intimidating but also intriguing, and so I read about it (for example, *How to Meditate,* by LeShan) but could never bring myself to practice it. Recently, however, I read Benson's *The Relaxation Response,* and because the word *meditation* was discreetly abandoned, I decided to give it a go. "Relaxation response" I could relate to. Well, I have been doing it fairly regularly ever since, and I am very pleased with the results. For one, it is very effective in reducing stress, as Benson amply documents. This may not be as significant to you now as it will be later, because I think young people have a greater tolerance for stress compared to older adults. On the other hand, I suspect that because young people have not been taught how to cope with stress, they frequently turn to drugs (including alcohol). Now is the time to learn to tune in to your body to discover what is really going on and to develop strategies for stress reduction.

Another reason I enjoy meditation is that it puts me in touch with my innermost self. I am convinced that this is where our creativity hangs out, and that meditation is a way to gain access to it, as are dreams, journal keeping, and many other techniques McCarroll talks about. Remember, it was Socrates who told the young men (women weren't permitted) he was teaching: "Know thyself!" All wisdom begins with self-knowledge. Some would say it ends there, too.

Well, enough on the self for now. Read *The Relaxation Response*, and then try for a week or so the simple guidelines he gives for meditating. In summary:

1. Find a quiet place.
2. Select an object to concentrate on, such as a word (mantra) or symbol or image, but keep your eyes closed.
3. Empty your mind of all thoughts.
4. Find a comfortable position, preferably sitting with your back straight, and gradually work up to twenty minutes of meditation a sitting, twice a day.

Be careful, though, because meditation can change your life! To quote Elaine: "Meditation—the process of stilling the mind and discovering the kingdom within—is the first step on the spiritual path. It can be a rough path. The meditator usually stumbles into an awareness of the tensions in her body, the anxieties of her mind, the wounded and empty places in her heart."

Love from your relaxed father,
Dad

Term Papers—
The "Curse" of College Students

Dear Lili,

I would like to get back to the topic of writing this time, and more particularly, the "curse" of college students, writing term papers. I must confess to a certain ambivalence about requiring term papers at the college level. Too frequently the prospect of writing a term paper is so threatening that students cop out by illegally purchasing a ready-made paper from a ghostwriting organization, "borrowing" one from another student, or engaging in outright plagiarism (read "theft") of another person's published work. Much of the blame lies with ill-preparedness as a result of inadequate high schooling. Many students literally do not understand the immorality (not to mention illegality!) of plagiarism.

One of the reasons term papers are so intimidating is that students (and some professors) set too-high standards for themselves. The purpose of most term papers is to learn how to research a topic, organize information in a meaningful way, and write it up in a readable and intelligent fashion. The goal is not an original contribution to the field, nor is it a polished, publishable production.

Many good books have been written to help students develop the skills for good term-paper writing; *Writing Research Papers: A Guide to the Process,* by Weidenborner and Caruso, is a good one. Some freshmen composition courses spend a couple of weeks describing the term-paper, or research-paper, process, and this coverage is usually very helpful. However, as with most skills, the way to learn is by doing. After writing a couple of term papers (and perhaps getting a few Ds and Fs!), you should get the hang of it, and from then on it won't be such an anxiety-ridden prospect.

One final word, and that is to warn against waiting-until-the-last-minute syndrome. This induces a panic situation that inevitably results in either a mediocre effort or it renders the dishonest way out as the only alternative. So, as the U.S. Postal Service advises, "start early and avoid the rush" (with library books as well as with your time!). Who knows? You may even enjoy writing a term paper!

Love,
Dad

Career Preparation

Dear Lili,

Well, Sweetheart, it's been a while since I have written to you, but I have been very busy of late. I went for a long walk today and had some thoughts about college and careers that I would like to share with you.

Too often, I think, students come to college with the idea that they will be taught what they need to know in order to succeed in a particular career or occupation. In a way it's true, but not in the way that they are assuming. What I mean is that the content of most of your courses, especially in fields like the sciences, will become obsolete in a very short time. Much more important than content is learning to organize your life. By this I mean a whole array of skills: how to think, how to concentrate, how to solve problems, how to ask questions, how to research, how to write reports, how to use a computer, and most important, how to learn! Once you learn that, you can learn anything.

At another level are the learnings that go on in the dorm: how to live with a stranger, how to judge character, how to pick and choose your friends, and finally, how to understand more about men and that wonderful mystery, sex.

Just the other day a student came to tell me about her experience of betrayal by a friend. She wasn't feeling well one day, so she asked her friend to withdraw some money from her checking account. She gave her friend her bank card, and somehow her friend succeeded in withdrawing an additional one hundred dollars for herself. It wasn't until the student received her monthly statement that she realized something was wrong. She suspected her friend but had no evidence. The bank promised to investigate, and with the threat of being discovered, the student's friend admitted that she took the money. She promptly returned it, with the excuse that it was purely an April Fool's joke. The student was quite hurt and felt betrayed. However, she thought about it and decided that she did not want to lose the friendship. She told her friend that she forgave her, still loved her, but that it was going to take time before she felt she could trust her again. She recognized that her friend was having some problems, both financial and personal. After hearing this story, I couldn't help being inspired by how the student had obviously learned a very important lesson in life. This was a lesson, she admitted, that she would never forget. Yes, learning takes place in the dormitory!

Lili, what I am trying to say is that college provides a transitional period between family and the world, when the students enter as "girls" fresh from the protective homes of middle-class America, and within a brief four-year period, a miracle occurs. The miracle is that they emerge as young women, mature, independent, self-assured, ready for the challenge that is theirs in a world that still discriminates against women but is slowly evolving into something very different.

I hope you can see that not all the lessons at college occur in the classroom. Maybe not even most of them.

Love,
Dad

Women's Day

Dear Lili,

I just want to tell you about two conferences I went to these past few days. On Wednesday I went to a conference at nearby Mercy College. The topic was "Women and Relationships." The keynote speaker was Nancy Friday of *My Mother/My Self* fame. She spoke on the topic of women and their expectations of men. I wish you could have been there. She gave a superb talk that seemed very much from the heart. She was genuine, thoughtful, attractive, and very tall. I think she mentioned being five feet ten inches, but she seemed even taller on an elevated stage.

What I want to tell you about is a study she conducted around the country with college students who were members of the class of 1981. She asked the women what messages they were communicating to the men in their life. Fully three-fourths of the women admitted to sending double messages. One message was the liberated, "I want to be your equal." The second was, "I want you to take care of me." More amazing was how the men received these double messages that were being sent. Only one-fifth of the men replied that they were getting the "I want to be taken care of" message. Do you suppose that is because the former message drowns out the latter, or do you think the young men were perhaps repressing, or not allowing themselves to hear, the "I want to be taken care of" message? Indeed, that's a pretty scary message to send to young men in this crazy world we live in today. No wonder they are not getting it!

The next day we at Marymount sponsored our second annual Women's Day, and the topic was "Health: Mental, Physical, and Social Dimensions." The keynote speaker was Jane Brody, personal health columnist for the *New York Times*. Ms. Brody gave an enthusiastic talk entitled "How to Get Well and Stay Well." She said that dieting without exercise is an exercise in futility, and I agree. She also seems to be opposed to vitamin supplements, assuming that you are getting sufficient dosages in your regular diet. Again I would agree, but I am not certain that college cafeteria food is always adequate, which is why I am always reminding you to take your vitamins (in moderation).

The workshop I went to in the afternoon was on anorexia. It was led by a student who introduced herself as a "recovered anorexic, although still in therapy." What an amazing young woman to get up in front of approximately thirty-five peers, faculty, and guests, and directly tell her story of struggling with anorexia nervosa since the age of fifteen. She was a dancer at the School of American Ballet, just like you, and suddenly she found herself on a downward spiral of losing weight. At first just five pounds, then another five, and then she couldn't stop until she was below eighty pounds and her parents became alarmed. Somehow she found the right therapist, one that she could respect and trust, and her weight (and life) began to turn around. She seemed so mature for her age that I couldn't help but wonder whether she had grown enormously as a result of this ordeal and the process of conquering it. Sometimes I suppose we have to learn the hard way, but at least she was learning! Everyone gave her a standing ovation when she had finished telling her story.

Well, Love, I thought you might be interested in what I have been up to lately. Never a dull moment in academia!

Love,
Dad

Writing Again

Dear Lili,

On the way back from the skiing weekend, I dropped off your class-mate Mandy. She told me that she wants to study journalism, and she asked for some advice. The best advice I could give her was to begin writing and never stop. As I said before, writing is a skill, and as with most skills, it requires discipline and practice.

In answer to her question, "Write about what?" I suggested that she keep a daily journal and write about her experience of the day. Learning to capture the day's tenuous moods and subtle nuances in words is a great discipline. It's what every writer must learn to do no matter what kind of writer he or she becomes.

Keeping a daily journal also helps to get in touch with one's inner life, and that is where I think true creativity resides. A kind of virtuous circle is established: keeping a journal helps you gain better self-understanding, which in turn makes you a better writer, which in turn helps you to understand yourself better, and so on. Every good writer recognizes that self-knowledge is essential to the craft of writing. You will remember that Ira Progoff has developed an elaborate technique of self-therapy through the use of a journal. It's called the Intensive Journal, and it makes explicit what I think many writers have had to learn to do implicitly through trial and error.

So, Dear Heart, if you want to become a good writer, remember the answer to the old joke about how to get to Carnegie Hall: "Practice! Practice! Practice!" But also heed the words of Socrates and "Know thyself!" So long for now.

Love,
Dad

College as Preparation for the Business World

Dear Lili,

I have just been thinking about how perfect college is, in many ways, for preparing you for the business world—in the broadest sense of the word *business*. Think of your teachers as managers under whom you are working. You have the opportunity to work for up to forty different managers with different personalities, styles, ages, sexes, races, religions, and so on. This is preparation for the work world! As you learn to be taught, directed, evaluated, disciplined—in a word, *managed*—so too you are learning valuable lessons for business. Also, as you learn to ask questions and negotiate about absences, grades, papers, you are learning the skills of the marketplace.

Just the other day, I had a confrontation with a senior over what appeared to be blatant procrastination in preparing for a class presentation. When she came to my office for advice, I accused her of not taking the course seriously, as evidenced by her letting everything go to the last minute. What impressed me most was the way the student handled the accusation. She kept her cool and explained, without becoming defensive, why her schedule had prevented her from beginning the work until now. She also explained that she always waits to the last minute, and that is just her style. When she left I felt badly and thought about what had occurred. What I realized is that I was projecting my own anxiety onto her. That night I wrote her a letter of apology, explaining how I had projected my anxiety instead of providing the support and respect that she deserved. The more I teach, the more I realize that good teaching is good management. I feel a lot closer to that student since the episode and apology. I suppose the lesson is that a good manager (and teacher) knows how to apologize.

Love,
Dad

College as Age-Segregated

Dear Lili,

I just wanted to convey an observation I made recently. I feel that most college-age young people are much too age-segregated in our society. When I or one of my colleagues visit one of the neighboring college bars, the reaction is occasionally one of, "Hey, you are invading our turf! This is a place only for young people." Ashley Montagu, a famous anthropologist, refers to this kind of attitude as ageism, a prejudice against the elderly. Montagu writes about how much he and his wife love to go dancing, but how frequently they are made to feel out of place whenever they go dancing in a place populated mostly by young people.

I notice an exception to this attitude among my Hispanic students, especially those from foreign countries. These students seem much more comfortable in the presence of older people, even people my age! I suspect it is because of their experiences with the extended family. In an extended family, young people are exposed to many situations involving people of all ages, and so they learn to be more comfortable. Also, I believe their experience of adolescence is less isolating than it is here. Anyway, I find my Hispanic students generally more friendly outside of class and more comfortable in social as well as academic situations.

Because you will be working mostly with older people when you graduate, I think it is important that you learn to overcome any shyness or prejudice toward people older than yourself. Now is the time to begin. Use your teachers and administrators as a way of working on this. There is no better antidote to ageism that I know of than making friends with older people and getting to know them better. You may even discover that they are not all that different from yourself!

Let me know what happens.

Love,
Dad

Guardian Angels
and Other Extraterrestrials

Dear Lili,

It all started with a discussion of Shirley MacLaine's best-selling book, *Out on a Limb,* in my general psychology class. The students found themselves challenged beyond credulity by MacLaine's arguments for reincarnation and the existence of extraterrestrials. At the same time, here at this women's college, they were flattered by the supposed extraterrestrial known as Mayan and her remarks to the effect that women are cleverer than men and need to believe in themselves as women. Incredulity, however, was the prevailing attitude of the students.

Feeling somewhat responsible to defend MacLaine's belief in extraterrestrials, I said, "Well, how about angels? Doesn't the Bible speak of angels? Besides, have not most of us been brought up with the idea of a guardian angel?" That was different they assured me, just a childhood belief that was no longer taken seriously. An angel is simply a metaphor for God's love and concern for us.

The discussion seemed to reach an impasse when a student in the back row raised a tentative hand. "Dr. Lawry, may I tell the class about something that happened to me last year?"

"Sure, Peggy, please rescue the class discussion," I pleaded gratefully.

In high school Peggy was a member of the field hockey team of a private school on the outskirts of Trenton, New Jersey. On days when the team played, Peggy usually received a ride home with her mother, because she would have to miss her bus. One day last year, Peggy's mother told her that she would not be able to drive her home, and that Peggy should arrange a ride home with a friend who drove. As fate would have it, Peggy's friend forgot, and Peggy was

43

stranded. Her aunt lived close by, so Peggy tried calling her, but to no avail—she was not home. The only route home was through a rough section of the inner city, so the prospect of walking home provoked some fear. But she appeared to have no choice, and Peggy embarked upon an anxious journey. Approximately halfway home Peggy rounded a corner and saw an old black man sitting on a park bench a few yards away. As she passed him, the old man looked up and said in a barely audible voice, "Don't be afraid, Peggy. Everything is going to be all right. You'll make it. You'll see." Startled and disbelieving her ears, Peggy replied, "Excuse me, what did you say?" The black man repeated his message. Immediately Peggy felt relieved and safe, though she puzzled over how he knew her name. As she approached the end of the street, Peggy noticed what looked to be a gang of teenage boys loitering and harassing passersby. She turned a different way to circumvent the block, and as she turned, her gaze drifted back to the park bench. The old black man had disappeared.

The second half of the journey was uneventful, but Peggy told the class that she will never forget that man and his message of "Don't be afraid." A tense silence was broken by the ringing of the bell. Class was over, but the question of guardian angels was not, except for Peggy.

Have you seen any guardian angels lately, Lil?

Love,
Dad

Taking Good Care (of Yourself)

Dear Lili,

I want to talk about taking good care of yourself again. I see so many students jeopardizing their health through a combination of alcohol, insufficient sleep and exercise, poor diet, and dependence on caffeine. One of the most important ways we take good care of ourselves is through good nutrition. It is only recently that I have begun to be aware of and to study good nutrition. Until then I simply opened my mouth and ate what was in front of me, with very little consciousness of what was healthy.

I suppose it was a chance encounter with someone almost exactly my age who almost died from cancer that woke me up. Jorgen, a medical doctor, told me that he had been given a few months to live because of cancer of the liver. He turned to the Hippocrates Institute in Boston, founded by Ann Wigmore. This grand old woman, sometimes called the mother of sprouting, has developed a very unusual approach to healing through nutrition. The approach is summed up in a famous quote from the ancient Greek physician Hippocrates: "Let food be your medicine and medicine be your food."

This approach to healing and health care is twofold. It radically changes the diet, and it also improves the elimination system through cleansing, detoxification, and a maintenance program.

The most radical and controversial aspect of the diet is that all the food is eaten raw (or "uncooked," as Jorgen prefers to say). Other requirements include:

- no caffeine (no coffee, tea, or caffeinated soda)
- only fresh fruit before lunch (as much as you want)
- never mix protein with starches or fruit
- no meat, fish, or dairy products (protein is obtained by eating a variety of nuts, seeds, and legumes)

- drink at least one ounce of wheatgrass juice every day, and eat lots of sprouts
- no salt, and no desserts with refined sugar

The rationale is that we have been so exposed to toxins in our food, air, and water that we must overcompensate with our food in order to detoxify our system. The experience of detoxification may be somewhat unsettling at first, causing headaches and constipation, but most people after a few days embark on an ascending curve toward robust health. In fact, to the extent you begin to clean up your diet, you should begin to experience more energy than you have had in a long time.

As for the elimination part, Frank, a colonic specialist and assistant to Jorgen, said that the worst colons he has seen are in young people who were born after World War II. Crohn's disease (a chronic form of inflammatory bowel disease) used to be a very rare disease, but it is appearing more frequently in young people. Junk food really takes its toll! For some a colonic therapy may be indicated in order to get the system operating at near maximum efficiency. However, for most young people, just cleaning up the diet and eating more fiber-filled foods (and fewer processed ones) will begin the detoxification process that includes the digestive and eliminative systems.

I began by restricting breakfast to fresh fruit. I usually eat melon or grapefruit the first thing and then have a banana sometime in mid-morning. Surprisingly, I experienced no loss of energy. Then, I eliminated coffee and tea, occasionally substituting herbal tea. Next, I cut out meat, and now I am in the process of reducing my consumption of cooked food, dairy products, and dessert. (Yes, Lil, I have become a confirmed vegetarian and have lost all desire for meat, though I still eat fish several times a week; I never thought it could happen to me, the inveterate meat eater.) I am working gradually toward the ideal outlined above, and I can already see and feel the effects.

I recognize that this approach to eating may be unrealistic in terms of what is available in a college cafeteria. But I feel you can certainly implement some of the major suggestions. For example, eating fresh fruit in the morning rather than frozen orange juice is a good place to start. Why? Because frozen juice is pasteurized, and as a result the enzymes are destroyed and so is a substantial amount of the vitamin C. Other suggestions would be large salads for lunch with seeds (sunflower, pumpkin, sesame) and nuts for protein and lemon juice for a dressing. The less oil the better. For snacks stick with fresh fruit or vegetables. Sugared snacks are a real downer and deplete your energy. Finally, I urge you to begin to cut down on meat consumption, especially red meat. You can get the necessary amount of protein in many other ways, and some nutritionists are beginning to say that we Americans are consuming too much protein. The important thing to remember is to begin slowly and allow yourself some time for adjustment. The way you begin to feel should be the most positive reinforcer and should therefore keep you motivated and protect you from discouragement.

One final word: Jorgen suggests that you keep a record of what you eat during a day and look it up in the *Nutritional Almanac* to be sure you are getting the necessary combinations of nutrients (including vitamins and minerals) for sustenance. As Jorgen says, we feed our cars better than we feed our bodies. We wouldn't think of putting leaded gas into a car that requires unleaded, and yet look at the junk we put into our mouth, frequently without knowing what its contents are!

I realize that it is difficult to relate to this because you are young and vigorous, and we are talking about an investment that probably won't pay its largest dividends for another twenty to thirty years. You will just have to take it on faith for the time being that it really is worthwhile. As a woman, of course, you have the additional incentive of prospective motherhood and providing your future children with the best maternal environment possible. But beyond all this, the tremendous way you begin to feel is immediate reward enough. Ultimately, we are responsible for our own health, which is what I want to pursue in my next letter.

Till then, Sweetheart.

Love,
Dad

Drugs and Medication

Dear Lili,

Recall that I ended my last letter with the idea that we are responsible for our own health. This is obviously true by virtue of monitoring what we eat, but it is also true of being careful of drugs and medication.

As for illegal drugs like marijuana and cocaine, I feel that to use them is like playing Russian roulette. We never know how our body is going to react to them. Remember the famous case of Karen Ann Quinlan—a combination of alcohol and illegal drugs led to a coma from which she never recovered. I recognize that the temptation to experiment is strong, and the chances are that you will, but don't be so foolish as to begin using drugs (including alcohol) as a way of coping with personal problems. I'll never forget the day a senior walked into my office a few days before graduation to apologize for her erratic attendance and performance in one of my classes. "I just wanted you to know, Dr. Lawry, that I am an alcoholic, but I have just joined Alcoholics Anonymous and am finally getting some help." My heart went out to her, and I hope she "recovered," because apparently there is no cure for alcoholism. Whenever personal problems arise, try the counseling center rather than the local bar. That's what counseling centers are for.

My other concern is legal medication. I tell my students that whenever they are given any medication, they should always look it up in the *Physicians' Desk Reference,* also known as the PDR, which should be available in the college library. The PDR will give you all the information you need to take medication prudently. For example, it lists all of the known side effects that may develop. It will also tell you what is contraindicated when using particular drugs—activities such as driving, drinking alcohol, and so on. Unfortunately, doctors do not always take the time to provide this information.

I am so adamant about this because I have a very good friend, Sheila, who was being prescribed Mellaril for psychotic episodes. After being on the drug for a period of time, she began to notice that her eyesight was getting worse. She went to an ophthalmologist for an examination, and he asked if she was on any medication. When she mentioned the Mellaril, he told her to consult with her psychiatrist. Sheila became suspicious and looked it up in the PDR. What she discovered horrified her. She was being prescribed a dosage that was greater than the maximum recommended by the manufacturer. Furthermore, she learned that one of the deleterious side effects of the drug is irreversible deterioration of the retina. When she finally confronted the psychiatrist about the dosage, he said simply that he was "treating patients, not running a drug seminar." He refused to give her an answer for what he had done. Sheila is now legally blind and cannot leave the house at night without an escort. In case you are wondering, a malpractice lawyer told her that it was next to impossible for patients with a mental illness to win malpractice suits and advised her not to pursue it.

The point I am making is that ultimately we are the only ones responsible for our health. If we don't take good care of our bodies and they begin to deteriorate, we are the ones who are going to have to live with the effects of that neglect or abuse. The same is true of a doctor's mistake. Again, we are the ones who have to live with the mistake, not the doctor. So take responsibility for your health by eating well, exercising, getting enough sleep, managing the stress in your life, and staying away from drugs. In that way you should never get sick and have to go to the doctor. The body is designed to stay well, and, if you take sufficiently good care of it, it will. I don't want to sound boastful, but in the last twenty years of teaching, I have missed only one day of class due to illness. I honestly believe that is how it should be.

So take care of that wonderful and mysterious body of yours, and avoid drugs like the plague, because that is what they are.

Love,
Dad

Learning What Really Matters:
Forgiveness

Dear Lili,

I am reading a fascinating book by Bernadette Roberts, an ex-nun, called *The Path to No-Self,* which contains the following paragraph:

> After two years at the university, I suddenly realized I had not learned a thing. Despite the influx of information, nothing had really happened, I was the same person with the same mind—I had not grown at all. If learning could not bring about change, if it was not a way of growth, then the university was a waste of time.

This induced a pang of guilt in me when I read it. Unfortunately, it expresses a sentiment that is not uncommon among students, and I was reminded of an experience that I had last year.

When I admitted at a party that I taught psychology, a number of people recollected how disappointed they had been with the psychology courses they had taken in college. "I always thought that psychology was supposed to be about life," one young woman remarked. "Boy, was I disillusioned." I took seriously the challenge implied in these remarks, and decided that my general psychology course this past fall was going to be practical if nothing else.

In addition to a standard text in the field, I introduced my students to a book that has had a powerful effect on my life recently, *Love Is Letting Go of Fear,* by Gerald Jampolsky. Jampolsky is a psychiatrist who specializes in working with children with catastrophic illnesses. Instead of reserving discussion of the book until the end of the semester, as I had done in the past, I decided to assign a lesson a week. The second of twelve lessons in the book is, "Forgiveness Is the Key to Happiness." Jampolsky says, "Inner peace can be reached only when we practice forgiveness."

During the class discussion of the lesson, I pointed out the significance of the word *only*. Jampolsky seemed to be saying that forgiveness is a necessary condition of inner peace, which is certainly a radical contention. At the end of the class, I suggested that everyone take Jampolsky's statement as a hypothesis to be tested and work toward forgiveness with someone in their life to see if peace would emerge.

At the beginning of the next class, I asked if anyone was successful in experiencing forgiveness toward someone. A very shy student in the first row raised her hand and began to tell the class what had happened between her and her older sister.

"My sister and I have not spoken for over two years because of a personal reason. I felt I was living in hell for those two years because I didn't feel comfortable when she came to visit. When she called on the phone, I would hang up when I recognized her voice. I missed her during that time, but I know now, thanks to Jampolsky, that I was afraid of being emotionally hurt again. This interfered with my forgiveness of my sister. Finally, after reading this lesson, I realized that by forgiving my sister, I would have peace with my family as well as with myself. I knew what I had to do. When I began to dial her number, I felt my hands shaking. When she answered she was just as shocked as I was that we were actually speaking to each other, and she began to cry. She could not believe that I had called her because she thought that she had hurt me so badly that there was no hope for our relationship. So, my sister and I made plans to speak to each other again after two years, and I confided to her that the reason I called was because of the book we read in class."

When the student had finished her story, a sudden transformation occurred in the room. We all knew something miraculous had happened, and we were privileged to witness it. I was reminded of a quote from *A Course in Miracles:* "The holiest of all the spots on earth is where an ancient hatred has become a present love."

At the end of the semester, I asked the students to write a reaction paper to Jampolsky's book. More than half of the students chose to write about the lesson on forgiveness. Almost everyone found the book practical, and most said that it had changed their life. I am most indebted to Dr. Jampolsky for helping to make my general psychology course something more than "a waste of time." It proves that college can be an opportunity for change and growth, but you have to be willing to take risks. Do you have anyone in your life who needs to be forgiven?

Goodbye, Sweetheart, I have to run for class!

Love,
Dad

The Spiritual Life

Dear Lili,

Today I would like to discuss the spiritual life with you. I know this is a topic you are not sympathetic to, and I don't want to confuse it with going to church on Sunday. I'm talking about something much more profound.

Fr. William McNamara, in his book *The Art of Being Human,* asks the blunt question of whether we are becoming saints. If not, he says, only one alternative exists—to become "failures." In the book *The Path to No-Self* that I mentioned in my last letter, Bernadette Roberts says simply that everyone (Christian or not) is called to a contemplative life, a life of prayer. This is the significance of the first so-called Great Commandment: To know and love God with our whole mind, heart, and strength. This is the purpose of life!

I know that is difficult to hear right now. Adolescence is a period of rebellion, and your childhood concepts of God and religion have to be rebelled against in order for you to arrive at a mature adult faith.

It may come as a shock to you to hear that loving God and your neighbor is the purpose of life, when your attention is focused on education and career preparation. But I ask you not to forget this when it comes time to make decisions about careers and, eventually, employment sometime in your senior year.

If what I have said is true, then it is very important that you ask for guidance from the Holy Spirit as to what you should be doing with your life. Believe it or not, this is the advice I give to seniors who are agonizing about what they are going to do after graduation. I tell them to pray and to ask for guidance (taken together, these actions are technically known as discernment) from the Holy Spirit. Those who take the advice are usually given some sign of what they are supposed to do. The results of discernment frequently surprise us, because we do not always know what is best for us (and what is best for us is what the Holy Spirit wants for us).

I remember a student who got the message in prayer that she was not supposed to marry the man to whom she was currently engaged. It was a very difficult decision, but she eventually broke off the engagement. Shortly thereafter she discovered how dishonest her fiancé had been with her.

Once we are in harmony with God's will, everything becomes much easier. It's a lesson that took me a long time to learn, but I think I've finally learned it. My life is much more peaceful now.

Peace be with you,
Dad

Making Friends with Your Shadow

Dear Lili,

I want to tell you about a fascinating exercise we did in general psychology today. I was talking about Carl Jung's theory of personality and his concepts of the persona and the shadow. According to Jung, the persona is the self we present in public, the mask we wear in our everyday encounters with others, the parts of our self that we have owned and integrated. The persona is who we want others to see and love.

On the other hand, the shadow is the dark side of the personality. We find it unacceptable, and therefore we have not integrated it into our perception of ourselves. Rather, we tend to project our shadow onto others and judge them adversely as a result. Although Jung says that the shadow is "90 percent gold," we usually don't believe it until midlife, if ever.

To get back to the exercise, in order to illustrate Jung's concepts of persona and shadow, I asked the class to take a sheet of paper and list all the qualities that best describe themselves, how they see themselves. Next, I asked the students to turn the paper over and list all the characteristics that they find most irritating in others, the things that really turn them off and make them not like the other person. When they had completed their lists, I told them that the first list of characteristics constituted their persona, and that the second list constituted their shadow.

I wish you could have seen their faces when I explained the significance of the lists. It was as if they had received a whole new insight into themselves. For example, one student listed generosity on the first list and selfishness on the second. I suggested to her that most of us who have not yet been canonized are a combination of generosity and selfishness. We have times when we are selfish, even though we may not be able to admit it to ourselves. Rare indeed is the person who is always generous or always selfish. I suggested further that the reason she finds selfishness in others so infuriating is that she has not yet accepted her own selfishness. Once she does, other people's selfishness won't be so upsetting. To prove it, I asked her if she had any negative qualities on her first list. She said, yes, she had listed awkwardness. I asked her if she found awkwardness in others irritating. She said she didn't. Obviously she has made peace with her own awkwardness and does not need to project it onto others.

It would seem that once we begin to integrate the shadow part of our personality, we not only become more whole, we also become less judgmental and more understanding. In fact, Jung writes that it is the work of the second half of our life to begin integrating the shadow in order to become self-actualized, or individuated, as he called it.

So, Lil, the next time you find yourself becoming really irritated with one of your classmates or teachers, check yourself and see if you can't honestly admit that perhaps the very thing you are condemning in someone else is something that you are, in fact, condemning in yourself.

I hope you find this concept helpful and that it gives you a way of working on yourself that is very positive and constructive. This is what maturity in the best sense of the word is all about. It's not simply about growing older; it takes a lot of courage and hard work. Just think, if you begin integrating your shadow ("making friends" with it), you might be ready for canonization by age fifty! Seriously, I firmly believe that we all have a calling to holiness, and this is an example of how modern psychology can contribute to that end. Jung is someone you might want to put on your lifetime reading list. He and Freud are probably two of the most important psychologists of the twentieth century. So try it, and let me know what happens!

To your shadow with love,
Dad

The Secret of Getting A's

Dear Lili,

I just want to get back to the number-one concern on the list that I mentioned at the beginning of the semester, namely, self-discipline. The biggest secret about discipline, as far as course management is concerned, is anticipation. Successful students anticipate—they are one chapter ahead of the professor rather than one (or more!) chapters behind, constantly playing catch-up. Having read the material before the professor's lecture, they have a frame of reference that makes the lecture meaningful. Frequently, when you haven't already read the material in advance, you literally do not know what the professor is talking about.

When it comes to performance in a typical college course, my theory is that study skills differentiate students more than anything else—more, perhaps, than intelligence or motivation. I believe that for most college courses, a student of average ability can get an A with good study skills. And paramount among good study skills is learning to anticipate the professor by keeping one chapter (or book or article) ahead. Granted, this takes a lot of discipline.

Related to this, of course, is attendance. Good study skills imply coming to class. As you have probably discovered already, getting someone else's notes is not even a reasonable facsimile of having been in class yourself. In a course like statistics, I estimate that it takes roughly triple the time to learn the material on your own (with the best notes) that it takes with regular attendance. Cutting class is very poor economy of time.

So, you want to get all A's! Don't miss any classes, take good notes, stay one chapter ahead of the professor, and turn assignments in on time. The rest should be easy!

Now I'll say something about the cardinal sin of procrastination. When students do not get a good grade in my courses, if it is not due to severe absenteeism, it is due to procrastination—waiting until the last possible minute to write a paper or to study for a quiz or an exam.

How do you avoid procrastination? I find the following suggestions most helpful:

- Get an early start. Think of it as working up to twenty-four hours ahead of yourself, and then it is just a matter of maintaining the status quo.
- Make two time schedules: one for the semester and one for the day. As soon as you are informed of the deadlines in your various courses, insert them in your semester schedule so that you can see what's coming up. I can't tell you the number of times students have told me that they forgot about a quiz date or a term paper deadline, even though it was listed on the syllabus distributed on the first day of class.
- Aim to complete tasks a few days earlier than they are due. This way, if for some unforeseen reason you miss the early self-imposed deadline, you still have time to meet the real deadline. Students have a lot of trouble dealing with contingencies like illness when they use a last-minute approach.
- Reward yourself for meeting your own deadlines. This is a form of behavior modification that you can utilize to manage your own behavior. Not only is there an inherent reward—anxiety relief—once a task is completed on time, but now there is an additional incentive. Psychologist B. F. Skinner demonstrated that behavior is pretty much a result of what he calls reinforcement (he feels the word *reward* is not scientific enough) and that there is no reason why you shouldn't use this principle toward regulating and changing your own behavior. By "reward" I mean anything that reinforces behavior or makes it more likely to occur the next time, like a treat (preferably sugarless!), a movie, watching a favorite TV program, going to a party, and so on.
- Take some quiet time and meditate. See if you get in touch with any resistances to the task that may be working against you unconsciously. If so, work toward eliminating them. For example, I see in many students a lot of resistance, based on fear, to giving presentations in class. Because the resistance is unconscious and unacknowledged, it operates to subvert the students' best intentions.

Such resistance manifests in surprising ways. One student fell on the stairs on the way to class on the day she was to give her presentation. Another student developed laryngitis the day before her presentation was due. It's very important to become aware of these resistances so you can begin to overcome them.

Well, Lil, I hope that gives you some ideas on using your time better. Remember that time is one of the most precious things we have, and learning to budget your time is one of the most important skills to be perfected in college. By the time you graduate, you should be finding many more hours in the day than you do now!

Love,
Dad

"Don't Sweat the Small Stuff"

Dear Lili,

A *Time* cover story on stress several years ago included a quote from cardiologist Robert Eliot: "Rule No. 1, don't sweat the small stuff. Rule No. 2, it's all small stuff." I'm sure you have discovered by now just how stressful college life can be if you don't manage it properly. But let's begin with a definition. Hans Selye, an expert on stress, defined stress as a nonspecific demand made upon the body. Selye observed that not all stress is harmful; in fact, we apparently need some stress to maintain normal functioning. Selye introduced the terms *eustress,* to connote good stress, and *distress,* to connote bad stress. The point is that much of the difference between good and bad stress has to do with perception and magnitude. For example, as I perceive it, rock music is *dis*tressful, but as you perceive it, it might well be *eu*stressful.

This reminds me of a study that was done a number of years ago on the effect of different kinds of music on plant growth. Using the same plants under controlled conditions, researchers tested the influence of rock, country, Indian raga, and classical music on the growth of plants. They found that rock music stunted growth and country music had no measurable effect either way, whereas Indian raga and some classical music (for example, Bach, but not Debussy) significantly improved growth to the point that plants leaned toward the speakers by as much as 60 degrees.

As for stress and magnitude, it's a matter of too much of a good thing being hazardous to your health. For example, winning a lottery has been known to cause a stroke or a heart attack. Some people seem to thrive on stress, and these people Selye calls race horses. Others seem to be able to handle only relatively small doses of stress. These Selye calls turtles. It's very important to know where you fall on this continuum of race horses and turtles. I suspect I am more of a turtle, whereas your mother is definitely a race horse. I feel you are somewhere in between, though I fear you tend to emulate your mother. (Just kidding!)

A number of areas contribute to the stress in one's life. Time management, which I talked about in my last letter, is one of them. Things get very hectic at exam time in college because of poor time management, over and beyond the normal test anxiety. Other major factors in our stress level are our eating, sleeping, and exercise habits. In addition to maintaining good nutrition habits, just eating three meals a day—especially breakfast—at regular times is a big help in keeping stress down. Also, the avoidance of alcohol, tobacco, caffeine, and other addictive drugs is a plus. Getting seven to eight hours of sleep is a factor. You know what happened at finals last semester when you pulled an all-nighter and practically blew the exam! Finally, exercising two to three times a week to the point of perspiration for a minimum of twenty minutes is also essential.

These areas, in combination, make up what we call our lifestyle. We can determine whether we possess a lifestyle that is healthy or unhealthy. I would say that the average college student has an unhealthy lifestyle, and that is why there is so much illness on campus (especially at exam time), in spite of the fact that the typical college student is at an age when the body is in its prime. A college environment produces a great many situational causes of stress that are unavoidable: living away from home for the first time; having a complete stranger as a roommate; spending long hours sitting in class, in your room, or in the library; taking exams and writing papers that will be graded and criticized; interacting with members of the opposite sex; handling your own money and not always having as much as you would like or as much as your friends have. I'm sure you could tell me about many others. Put all these situational causes of stress together with an unhealthy lifestyle and you have the potential for a very lethal combination somewhere along the line.

College is a kind of microcosm of the real world and a training ground, so to speak, for adult society. It is a wonderful invention for assisting in the difficult transition from child to adult in our culture. It used to be that high school performed that function, but that ended with the generation of your grandparents. Now the majority of young people at least begin college, although far from all graduate. When they don't graduate, it has more to do with lifestyle and stress management choices than it does with intelligence or ability. However, you should keep in mind that there is probably some relationship (though this is not a hard and fast rule) between intelligence and lifestyle. In other words, I believe that intelligent people take better care of themselves, all things being equal. At the same time, a lot of intelligent people are "killing" themselves. I am sure you know some.

So that's my rap on stress management and lifestyling. I hope I am not being an unheeded prophet in my own home and that you will be able to heed some of your father's advice!

Take good care.

Love,
Dad

My Graduate School Mentor

Dear Lili,

Do you recall the letter I wrote about getting the "right" courses? I mentioned that it is good to choose your courses by the professors who teach them as much as by the subject. The best teachers love their subjects, and they love their students. If you were to ask a few seniors who the best teachers are, the best would be the ones whose names come to nearly everyone's lips without needing to think about it.

I had such a teacher when I was a graduate student at Duquesne University, where I spent two years in the master's program in general psychology. That teacher's name is Dr. David Smillie. He was a professor of developmental psychology. I will never forget him.

Dr. Smillie was one of the first true intellectuals I had ever encountered in my formal education. Many of my other teachers were good secondary sources and bridges to original thinkers, but Dr. Smillie was the first truly *original* thinker I had had as a teacher. It was a joy to sit in his classroom because you knew you were hearing things that weren't written down anywhere else, things that hadn't come from someone else's book. When I first sat in on one of his lectures, I thought to myself, "Now *this* is what graduate school is supposed to be about!" Needless to say, he was brilliant. But he was also a good communicator and a very effective teacher. I had no doubt that he loved his subject, and that enthusiasm was infectious.

I became so enamored with the subject of developmental psychology that I decided to do my master's thesis in that discipline. I asked Dr. Smillie to be my thesis advisor. He agreed, and invited me into his doctoral-level seminar on Jean Piaget, the great Swiss cognitive psychologist. I was only a master's-degree candidate, so this was a most flattering invitation. That seminar on Piaget taught me how to read in a way that no other course in my academic career had done. To begin with, Piaget is very difficult to read, but the fact that we were reading him in an English translation from the French made it even more difficult. We used as our texts several of Piaget's books, such as *Play, Dreams, and Imitation in Childhood* and *The Origins of Intelligence in Children*. These are now classics in the field, but they were not as well known back then.

Because it was a small seminar, all of us were encouraged to do a little reading of very difficult texts and to participate in a lot of discussions. But what I remember most about the course was that I was in the presence of a teacher who read a book by an intellectual giant like Piaget *on his own terms*. It was like watching a dramatic re-enactment of a real-life dialog between Piaget and one of his colleagues. Dr. Smillie modeled a way of reading and thinking that I had never been exposed to before. It was a graduate student's dream course!

There is no question that Dr. Smillie was brilliant and that he loved his subject, but what about his love for students? I must confess that Dr. Smillie was not a particularly charismatic teacher. He certainly did not possess the kind of personality that easily seduced and drew in his students. On the other hand, he was always pleasant in the classroom, and he held an annual party for all his students—both graduate and undergraduate—at his home. This at an institution where caring was very much in fashion demonstrated more than the usual care that graduate professors had for their students.

The thing I remember most, however, is how he gave positive feedback to a student when he thought that the student had done a particularly good job. I will never forget Dr. Smillie's words of congratulations and praise to me after I presented my thesis proposal for the first time in a thesis seminar. His words were straightforward, for Dr. Smillie could never be accused of hyperbole, and the feelings behind them were genuine. His compliments were real, and they were never given lightly. That brief encounter was one of the highlights of my career as a graduate student. It taught me the power of a timely and well-placed word of encouragement or a brief compliment such as, "Well done," especially when it comes from someone in authority who is respected and well liked.

I recall a story about Jimmy Johnson, former coach of the Dallas Cowboys. Johnson led the Cowboys out of last place to win the 1993 and 1994 Super Bowls. He was often asked about what he had done to effect such a change in the team. He felt that one element of the change had to do with his attitude toward rookie players during training camp. These young players are among the best in the country, as evidenced by the fact that they have been picked by a professional team. Although they are among the elite, they do not know if, in the end, they will make the team or be sent home to seek more conventional employment. To allay the rookies' fears and anxieties, Johnson made a point of learning each rookie's name, calling him by name, and commenting on the good things the player did at practice. Many coaches wait until the squad has been cut before they even *try* to learn the new players' names, but Johnson believed that his attention to young players could be a deciding factor in whether the players made the team.

This story reminds me of something that occurred the first year I taught at Marymount. A senior faculty member, a man quite well known in his field, invited me to lead his senior honors seminar in a discussion of Rollo May's *Existential Psychology*. I was a bit intimidated by the reputation of these honors students, not to mention by the famous professor in charge. Still, I approached the seminar with a lot of enthusiasm—after all, I had just received my master's degree from Duquesne University, one of the few existential-phenomenological psychology programs in the country.

Somehow, we got onto the topic of the importance of teachers knowing the names of their students. I had read *The Art of Teaching*, by Gilbert Highet, the summer before, and I made a strong case for the importance of knowing students' names. I cited Highet as my authority—he tells a devastating story about the famous poet A. E. Housman, who would *boast* of his inability to remember his students' names. (I have since been reminded by the writing of Robert Perry that the Good Shepherd in John's Gospel knew his sheep by name.) The famous professor, however, argued vigorously against the importance of knowing students' names; and later in the discussion, it suddenly become apparent that he did not even know all the names of the twelve or so students in the seminar—and it was well into the semester! The moment was embarrassing, but it taught me that not all discourse at the university is objective and rational.

But to get back to my graduate school mentor: I have never forgotten the lesson taught me by Dr. Smillie's generosity, and I try to praise and congratulate my own students as much as possible. His example speaks to me of the power of a teacher to influence not only one's own students but even one's students' students! I suppose that is what is meant by the "spiral of love." It just keeps increasing.

May you be so blessed to find such a teacher!

Love,
Dad

Letters to Daughters

Dear Lili,

Letters of advice from parent to child have been around for a long time, and they constitute a substantial genre in literature, including Lord Chesterfield's famous letters to his son. Among other examples is Charlie Shedd's beautiful *Letters to Karen,* a compilation of personal letters *On Keeping Love in Marriage,* as the subtitle describes it. Perhaps less well known are the letters of F. Scott Fitzgerald to his daughter, Scottie, when she was a boarding student in high school and later at Vassar, class of 1942. Though the language is a bit quaint, I see much wisdom and prophecy in what Fitzgerald had to say to his adolescent daughter. Therefore, I have gleaned a few paragraphs that I judged to be worth listening to:

> For premature adventure one pays an atrocious price. As I told you once, every boy I know who drank at eighteen or nineteen is now safe in his grave. The girls who were what we called "speeds" (in our stone-age slang) at sixteen were reduced to anything they could get at the marrying time.

> If you will trust my scheme of making a mental habit of doing the hard thing first, when you are absolutely fresh, and I mean doing the *hardest* thing *first* at the *exact moment that you feel yourself fit for doing anything* in any particular period, morning, afternoon or evening, you will go a long way toward mastering the principle of concentration.

> Certainly you should have new objectives now—this of all years ought to be the time of awakening for that nascent mind of yours. Once one is caught up into the material world not one person in ten thousand finds the time to form literary taste, to examine the validity of philosophic concepts for himself, or to form what, for lack of a better phrase, I might call the wise and tragic sense of life.

Well, Lil, how's that for some sage advice that has a contemporary ring to it, though written over half a century ago? (Fitzgerald died in 1940 at the young age of forty-four—perhaps we can infer that he did not take much of his own advice.) If you want to read all one hundred pages of them, and I recommend that you do, then look up *The Letters of F. Scott Fitzgerald*, edited by Andrew Turnbull.

By the way, just one last favorite quote from Shedd's *Letters to Karen*, because it inspired this book: "Marriage is not so much *finding* the right person as it is *being* the right person!"

That's all for now—I won't keep you any longer from the book I hope you are reading!

Love,
Dad

Poetry—The Food of the Soul

Dear Lili,

I want to encourage you to take some time to discover poetry while you are at college. I suppose the easiest way would be to take a course in poetry, but it should be with a very special teacher. F. Scott Fitzgerald said that Princeton had only one teacher of poetry while he was there, whereas some of the other professors who taught poetry actually seemed to hate it and not know what it was about.

I discovered poetry quite by accident. In my college freshman English literature class, I was randomly assigned the poet Alfred Lord Tennyson and told to become an "expert" on him and to give a presentation on him late in the semester. So I read everything I could get my hands on and eventually discovered *Idylls of the King,* Tennyson's verse rendition of the Arthurian myth. Reading that book was a major turning point in my education—I discovered great literature directly, a directness I managed to avoid in high school by using Cliff Notes and reading Classic Comics. I have been reading the Great Books ever since my encounter with Tennyson, though I do not read as much poetry as I would like.

I know now that Tennyson was a second-rate poet compared to Donne, the Brownings, Shakespeare, Keats, and many others. (As Fitzgerald said of Keats, "For awhile after you quit Keats all other poetry seems to be only whistling or humming.") Nevertheless, I cut my poetry teeth on Tennyson, and I will be forever grateful. In fact, I suspect that one may have to struggle a bit to really begin appreciating great poets like those I have mentioned. It is the same for classical music! It may be easier to begin with some contemporary poets. When I was your age, poets of the day were people like Ferlinghetti, Frost, Dickey, Baldwin, Prevert, and Ginsberg, to name a few. You could do worse than to start there, or with the recognized poets of your own generation. Remember that poetry is for your soul as much as for your mind.

I am sending you a copy of *The Pleasures of Poetry*, by Donald Hall, which is the best anthology of poetry from Shakespeare to the present day that I know of. It also contains an eighty-eight-page introduction to poetry that is quite brilliant and manageable. And if you want something more contemporary, find the excellent anthology by John Nims, *Western Wind: An Introduction to Poetry*. Read, savor, and enjoy!

Love,
Dad

Honest in Relationship

Dear Lili,

I want to tell you about a student who came to see me a little more than a year ago. It seems she had met a young man while studying abroad the year before and had fallen in love. After her return to the United States, the young man wrote of his desire to marry her. The dilemma my student was facing was whether to tell him that she has herpes. She was married before, at a very young age, and her husband had herpes, and eventually she got it. Her fear, of course, is that she will lose the young man she met in Europe when he learns of her disease. She asked me what she should do.

I told her to follow her heart, and she decided to write and tell him. Well, for the next few days, my student was a basket case waiting to hear from her beloved. As soon as she mailed the letter, she began to doubt the wisdom of her decision. She literally went through hell!

One day not long after, she came to my office with a big smile on her face. I knew the answer. Indeed, he called to say that his love transcended her herpes, and that it really didn't matter as far as his desire to marry her was concerned. I hugged her, and she danced out of my office transformed.

My reason for telling you this is primarily to impress upon you the importance of honesty in a relationship. It's hard to be honest sometimes, because we are afraid we might lose the other person if some difficult truth becomes known. The irony is that the truth usually becomes known, and, more often than not, it's not so terrible. Better in the long run to face the truth than to live a lie. If you are honest about who you are and the other person still loves you, then love is fortified. On the other hand, if you cannot be honest, then the relationship is always in jeopardy. Telling the truth builds trust, and trust is probably one of the most important characteristics of a good relationship. Nothing is more comforting than knowing that the other person will always be truthful no matter what. Can you imagine my student waiting until after she married to tell her husband she has herpes? What a terrible way to begin a marriage. So, tell the truth, Lili, no matter what. Remember, as the saying goes, a friend is someone who knows all about you and still loves you.

Love,
Dad

College:
"Gold Mine" or "Smorgasbord"?

Dear Lili,

Analogies and images often give us new and fresh ways to think about our experience. Life can be a "bowl of cherries" or a "mountain railroad" or a "piece of cake." Our day can feel like an uphill climb until we reach a point where "it's all downhill from here." Some relationships sour, and others blossom. Understanding marriages, friendships, careers, and even our time in·college can be enhanced by the use of analogies and images.

I'm thinking about all this because I just discovered a survey that I thought you might be interested in. It was conducted among the students of Saint Louis University, who were asked which of eleven images best described the university for them. Overall, the most popular was a tasty "smorgasbord" (21.9 percent), and the least popular was a "monastery" (1.1 percent). Freshmen concurred with the majority, choosing predominantly either "shopping center" or "smorgasbord," whereas older students chose "escalator" or "purgatory." Somewhere in the middle were the disenchanted, who chose "assembly line," and the confused, who chose "maze." Also in the middle were those who truly found a home and who recognized what a precious opportunity they had to be living for four years with relatively little responsibility—for these the university was a "gold mine."

If your experience of college so far is best described as a smorgasbord, or worse, a maze, I truly hope that you will discover its potential as a gold mine before you graduate. My suspicion is that most students do not realize what a gold mine college is until after they graduate and begin their journey in the "real world."

Perception is critical here. If you recognize the potential of college as a gold mine, then you will set about digging for gold. On the other hand, if college becomes nothing more than a maze or an escalator, then you will learn how to get through or to play the game with very little to show beyond the diploma. Your gaze will be fixed upon the goal, and as a result, you will never appreciate the process. And if you think about it, the process is all we really have. The goal may never come for those who drop out or for those who die before graduation, but everyone has the process, and it is all we have at the moment.

May the rest of your moments at college be golden, Sweetheart.

Love,
Dad

Prayer

Dear Lili,

I want to talk about prayer. I know that it's a subject we have never discussed before, and I suspect that it might be easier by letter.

Up until recently I suppose I have taken my prayer life for granted. As you know I now meditate (another name for prayer) for about twenty minutes in the morning, after doing some yoga exercises. I am also aware of your critical attitude toward meditation. Perhaps it's the word that is off-putting. It was for me for a long time, until I read Herbert Benson's *The Relaxation Response*. That book demythologized the word *meditation* for me like nothing else I had read. I realize now that the scope of Benson's book is very limited, but it was definitely the right book at the right time for me.

I said I have taken my prayer life for granted until recently—I am now taking a second look at my prayer as a result of being on an extended retreat. I have come to realize that prayer is nothing more than a word we use for tuning in to God. It can be done anywhere at any time, but sometimes it helps to be in a quiet place, sitting or kneeling. In fact this quiet time and space is a real salve for the nervous system, as Benson demonstrates, and may even be necessary for optimal psychological functioning.

But the real purpose of prayer, as I said, is tuning in to God— and in to God's plan for us. This is what we were created for. Nothing more or less. Christ said it many different ways, but this is my favorite, from the Gospel of John:

> "Remain in me, as I in you.
> As a branch cannot bear fruit all by itself,
> unless it remains part of the vine,
> neither can you unless you remain in me.
> I am the vine,
> you are the branches.

Whoever remains in me, with me in him,
bears fruit in plenty;
for cut off from me you can do nothing.
Anyone who does not remain in me
is thrown away like a branch
—and withers;
these branches are collected and thrown on the fire
and are burnt.
If you remain in me
and my words remain in you,
you may ask for whatever you please
and you will get it
It is to the glory of my Father that you should bear much fruit
and be my disciples.
I have loved you
just as the Father has loved me.
Remain in my love.
If you keep my commandments
you will remain in my love,
just as I have kept my Father's commandments
and remain in his love.
I have told you this
so that my own joy may be in you
and your joy be complete."

(15:4–11)

Just meditate on this for a while.

There are many ways to pray, but the one you discover instinctively is probably best for you. I believe the Holy Spirit guides us in these matters, and if you need help, that is what a so-called spiritual director is for. Once you begin to take your prayer life seriously, your whole life will begin to change. I challenge you to put your adolescent objections to religion and all the rest behind you and to renew your relationship with God through prayer. You will not be disappointed. "When you search for me, you will find me; if you seek me with all your heart, I will let you find me" (Jeremiah 29:13–14).

Love,
Dad

Beating Test Anxiety

Dear Lili,

I have been thinking about what you said on the telephone last night. I want to be sure that I gave you enough time to talk about the situation between you and your roommate. I suspect that I may not have, because I become anxious when I think that you are hurting, and I defend myself by telling you it's going to be all right and then changing the subject. I suspect you get the message that I don't want to (or can't) talk about it. Anxiety is a very insidious emotion, which brings me to what I really want to talk about in this letter.

One of the greatest obstacles I see interfering with performance in college is test anxiety. In technical terms, test anxiety happens when a person's level of arousal goes beyond its optimal point, with the result that performance suffers. To use an analogy, it is as if we experience our minds like a painter's palette, but all the colors are running together.

Level of Arousal and Efficiency of Performance

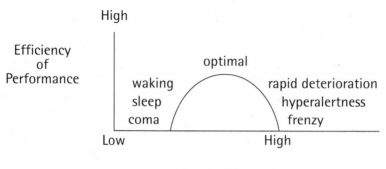

77

As you can see from the graph, a certain amount of arousal is needed to enhance performance. Otherwise we are dull and listless, too "laid back." Therefore, a certain amount of excitement (arousal) before any performance is actually helpful. It gets us "up" for the occasion. The challenge is to get to the optimal level without spilling over into hyperalertness or frenzy, where we become counterproductive. I suppose it is the difference between having the jitters before some performance and having stage fright, where it becomes incapacitating.

The best defense against test anxiety is being and feeling well prepared. I think much test anxiety is brought about by procrastination and unpreparedness. So, if you have studied well and feel fairly confident, half the battle with test anxiety is over.

Another suggestion is to meditate right before you take the test. Go to the chapel or your room (or any quiet place) and just clear your mind. Use a mantra if you find that helpful. Just keep repeating the affirmation, "I will pass the test with ease." Also, if you can visualize yourself having taken the test and done very well on it, that can be helpful as well. These techniques may sound a little hokey, but they really work!

Finally, I think it should be obvious that your mind functions better when your body is well rested. So whatever you do, do not stay up the night before the exam, but get a good night's sleep. Also, avoid stimulants like coffee before taking a test. The natural excitement will stimulate you enough without the addition of caffeine. So many times I have seen students bring coffee into an exam. I used to do it myself! Unfortunately, arousal is self-perpetuating (even addictive), and so you have to learn how to control it—otherwise it controls you.

As a postscript, remember to keep the test in perspective. Don't allow it to become more important than it truly is. Face the worst scenario (failing it), and ask yourself honestly what would happen if that occurred. I have seen too many students get so worked up over a relatively minor quiz that you would think their life depended upon it. Try these suggestions before your next test, and remember that a quiet mind is a powerful mind.

Love,
Dad

College: Is It Really Worth It?

Dear Lili,

I suspect the thought has crossed your mind as to whether all this hard work is really worth it. Let me share with you the results of some research I have done with regard to the impact of college on young people.

For one thing, just being a college graduate is special for someone of your generation. Even though slightly more than half of the people who graduated from high school in 1985 went to college (and slightly more young women than men did), far less will have attained a degree by 1989 or even later. (The best estimates are that between 35 and 50 percent drop out. It is a difficult statistic to gather because dropouts can always drop back in and graduate.) In fact, only one in five people age twenty-five to twenty-nine now has a college degree (much higher than one in seventeen, the figure in 1940). Furthermore, the gap in salaries between college graduates and high school graduates seems to be increasing! For example, the Census Bureau in 1983 found that the median income of male college graduates, age twenty-five to thirty-four, was 39 percent higher than for high school graduates. In 1979, the gap was significantly less, at 21 percent. (In 1997, that statistic is probably even more impressive as a trend. The bad news, according to a Bureau of Labor Statistics report, is that "at least 22 percent of all college graduates entering the work force between 1994 and 2005 were or will be either unemployed or in jobs for which a bachelor's degree is not ordinarily considered a necessity.") So, a college education may or may not have an impact on your future earnings, but salary potential should not be the only factor that motivates the pursuit of a college education. Speaking purely economically, your college education is a substantial investment (I estimate more than $50,000 before it's all over!), and it will take years before the salary differential compensates for the initial investment plus the loss of four years' income.

More important, a number of studies have been conducted on the impact of college attendance on the so-called nonintellective (cocurricular and extracurricular) variables. You may remember that this was the topic of my doctoral dissertation. I did a longitudinal study of the changes that students who persisted to graduation in 1970 underwent as a result of attendance at Marymount College. I found that students in general became more liberal (which no longer may be the case), more culturally sophisticated, more socially conscious, and more autonomous with regard to both family and peers.

It's interesting that in 1976, after surveying many such studies, a researcher by the name of Katz came up with the following list of areas of change for college students:

- decrease in authoritarianism, or relying on authority for definition
- increase in autonomy (same as my study)
- increase in self-esteem
- increase in the capacity for relatedness
- increase in political sophistication
- increase in aesthetic capacity
- development of a broader grasp of theoretical issues

I referred before to these changes as "nonintellective." This means that they do not have so much to do with increased knowledge and cognitive development, which should be automatic with more education. Nonintellective changes are more like by-products of a college education. They seem to happen alongside the more intellective changes that one would expect as a result of attendance at college. I think you would agree that the changes are, for the most part, positive ones. In fact, for my money they are truly the more important changes and therefore should distinguish the college graduate as not only learned but refined, sophisticated, and, hopefully, moral and wise as well.

Another way of saying this, Lil, is that a college education transcends its monetary advantage for its recipients by improving the quality of their life, both personally and occupationally. Indeed, it's not a panacea, and it doesn't benefit everyone equally. We must always remember Alexander Pope's caveat: "A little learning is a dangerous thing." But all things being equal, a person with a college education (not merely a degree!) is better prepared for the exigencies of life as well as for a career, and, therefore, I would like to believe, is a happier, more fulfilled individual as well. In fact, research has been done that suggests that education is positively related to happiness and mental health. The more you have of one (education), the more you are likely to have of the others (happiness and mental health)!

Well, Dear Heart, I want you to reflect on this, and please keep it in mind whenever you feel like throwing in the towel. It really is worth it!

Love,
Dad

Paying for College

Dear Lili,

I'm sorry that so much of our correspondence is taken up with money matters and forms to be filled out and signed, but that's the reality of college education today for most Americans.

In the survey I took of my class on things they had to learn about college that they wish someone had told them, "money problems" was second on the list. I was surprised, because it is something students rarely talk about (at least with professors), but apparently struggle with a great deal. These are some of the factors involved in the struggle.

First of all is the concern of their parents trying to meet the spiraling costs of college education today, especially in the private sector. This concern on the part of parents has to have some effect on the student. Though I try not to complain, I'm sure you pick up on my anxiety over meeting the bills.

Second is the worry about accumulating debt in the form of loans that will come due all too quickly after graduation. I estimate that your loans will amount to at least ten thousand dollars by graduation, and that is probably typical. This, coupled with the anxiety of getting that first job after graduation in order to begin making payment on the loans, is a double whammy.

Third is the reality that more and more students have to resort to part-time jobs in order to get by: working after school, on weekends, or through work-study grants, such as you have. By the way, I thought you might be interested in the fact that students who work under fifteen hours a week tend to do better in school than those who don't work at all! Apparently, students who work part-time learn to budget their time better and seem to appreciate their education more, because they are helping to pay for it.

Finally, I see a lot of stress in students who are not able to keep up with their friends in terms of clothes, going out, and so on, because of money problems. This can be very demoralizing, and it is not frequently discussed with anyone, out of a sense of pride and embarrassment. It is very difficult for a student to say, "I can't afford to go out with you guys tonight."

The best way to cope with money problems, short of winning the lottery, is to make out a budget. If you haven't learned to do this before, now is the time! Make up a list of all the expenses you anticipate other than tuition and board: books, fees, personal effects. Then make up a list of sources of income: work-study payments, allowance, baby-sitting, and so on. Total the two columns, and if the expenses come to more than the income, you are in trouble! More income obviously has to be generated (like more allowance!). On the other hand, if you have more income than expenses, then the difference becomes your discretionary fund, and this is the amount you have left over to spend on entertainment and other "luxuries." If you divide that figure by the number of weeks in the semester, you get some idea of how much you can afford to spend on extras on a weekly basis, and how you should plan your spending so that you don't end up short a few weeks before the end of the semester. I know it takes a lot of discipline to live on a budget, but it is important preparation for the reality you will be dealing with after you graduate, get your first job, and, presumably, move away from home. Nothing is worse than seeing young adults, single or married, riddled with financial debt because they have never learned this very important skill and lifetime habit. So start your budget today, and let me know what the bottom line says.

Goodbye for now, Love, and remember, "A penny earned is a penny saved."

Love,
Dad

Finding God in Nature

Dear Lili,

As you know, I am on retreat for three months during my sabbatical this term. This time has given me a chance to notice the extraordinary presence of God in the world through the phenomenon of continual change.

Each day I go for a walk in the surrounding woods, and I am amazed at how much things change from one day to the next. Having lived in the city most of my life, the reality of such change has escaped me. I think it takes a certain amount of time outdoors in nature every day to become aware of what I am talking about. By living so much of our life indoors and in automobiles, we are cut off from nature's constantly changing face.

Before, I could never understand people's passion for hiking, camping, and so on. It always seemed so inconvenient and a bit like trying to rediscover one's lost adolescence. I was a Cub Scout and a Boy Scout, and I camped out and hiked when I was supposed to. Why did I have to subject myself to all that discomfort as an adult? Still, people who work the earth have always seemed to me to be closer to God than city folks. No wonder many of the early saints of the church found God in the desert or up on the mountain! Now I am beginning to understand.

I think there is something very healthy and spiritual about spending lots of time outdoors communing with nature. I urge you to become familiar with this great outdoor cathedral. Try to schedule a walk every day, alone if possible. See if you can't get in touch with what I am talking about. I don't think it is coincidence that many of the popular sites of pilgrimage inspired by apparitions of the Blessed Mother—Fatima, Lourdes, Guadalupe, and others—are outdoors. God and the heavenly kingdom are definitely there in the birds, the trees, the water, the wind, the rocks, and most of all, the silence. You don't have to go to a church to find God, Lili. God is there right outside your window. All we have to do is learn again how to see and listen.

Love,
Dad

Self-Esteem, Attractiveness, and Ego

Dear Lili,

A friend of mine, Rita Jackaway Freedman, gave a lecture last night at Marymount entitled, "The Power and Burden of Feminine Beauty," based on her book *Beauty Bound*. The book explores the impact of physical attractiveness on women's lives and body-image problems. Rita described how life seems to be more kind to people who are judged to be physically attractive, from getting more hugs as babies to being better liked by classmates, teachers, and even juries. Unfortunately, the burden is far heavier for women than for men, because men in general have greater access to other things that compensate for the lack of physical attractiveness—things like power, status, and even beautiful women.

Recently, researchers Abloff and Hewitt found that another dynamic operates in perceived attractiveness, and that is self-esteem. In fact, self-esteem may be the primary dynamic, even more important than physical attractiveness. What they found is that we tend to prefer (be attracted to) people perceived as having relatively the same amount of self-esteem as ourselves. A number of variations are reported, but the one I think is most relevant has to do with people who are perceived as having higher self-esteem. If that person is male, people (both male and female) are attracted to him; but if the person is female, people in general tend not to be attracted to her.

I think this is important for you to know because I feel you project high self-esteem—if it is possible for a father to be objective about such matters concerning his own children, especially a daughter! According to this study, therefore, people will tend to avoid you through no fault of your own other than that you are female and have high self-esteem. I think it underlines how sexism is so ingrained in our society that it frequently operates on an unconscious basis.

Frankly, I don't know how to advise you to deal with this finding. To ask you to "turn down" your high self-esteem may be asking the impossible. It might also be counterproductive. It is important, however, to be aware of how others perceive us. Also, it is important to keep in mind that the study was conducted with college students. Hopefully we outgrow this tendency as we get older and wiser, just like we get beyond the importance of physical attractiveness!

I am reminded of how upset you were at around the age of twelve or thirteen, when you went to a birthday bowling party. You were the only girl at the party. After the first few frames, you started winning, and the boys began to harass you unmercifully. As a result your game deteriorated significantly, and I remember you asked me later why these boys, who were your friends, would do something so cruel. I tried to explain the vulnerability of the male ego, though I did not use those exact terms at the time. I think that was the first time you experienced sexism, or at least were aware of it. I felt sorry for you, but I knew it was something you would have to learn to deal with, just as you are learning to deal with the sexist remarks you hear in the classroom from your male classmates.

At times like this, I wonder if we made the right choice in sending you to sex-segregated elementary and high schools. However, I am comforted by the research of Winchel, Fenner, and Shaver, which shows that girls who went to all-girl schools somehow become immune to the "fear of success" seen frequently in girls who attend coed schools. So don't be discouraged, Sweetheart, and see this brand of sexism as another opportunity to grow and excel.

Love,
Dad

The Women's Movement: Passé?

Dear Lili,

I know you feel that most if not all the women's liberation battles have been fought and won, and that the women's movement is a bit passé. In fact, your generation has even been referred to as the post-feminist generation. I gave you a subscription to *Ms.* magazine in the hope that you would see just how naive that belief is. Most of my students do not discover the harsh realities of sexism until after they graduate and enter the job market. However, to the extent that you are informed of those realities before you graduate, I feel you are in a much better position to cope with them later.

Since I teach statistics, I'm afraid my argument is going to be predominantly statistical. For example, are you aware that the average woman in the United States is still making only about 70 percent of what the average man makes? That the average secretary (female) has two more years of education than the average male boss? That the average female with an MBA from Columbia University earns 19 percent less than her male counterpart ten years after she gets her degree?

When you look at the population beyond the United States, the figures are even more depressing. According to estimates and projections published by the United Nations, women represent 50 percent of the adult world population; make up one-third of the official labor force; earn 10 percent of the world's income (at least American women have made some obvious progress, but not as much as in other countries, such as Sweden); own only 1 percent of the world's property (there are still countries in the world, such as Saudi Arabia and Iran, where women are not permitted by law to own property); and grow 50 percent of the world's food (and the majority of female farmers do not get paid for their work). Furthermore, 30 percent of the households in the world are headed by women (only 11 percent of American families have two parents and at least one child!). Seventy percent of the world's illiterates are women. Finally, in developing countries, 70 percent of the women who work outside the home are in agriculture (mostly doing backbreaking work in the fields).

I find these statistics very shocking and depressing, and I hope you do, too. I am reminded of a story that was told to me by a U.N. representative who spoke at Marymount about the condition of women in the world. In order to make the point that in many countries women do not have much more status than a beast of burden, he recounted how donkeys were given to families in a particular village to ease the burden of the women who usually carried the heavy loads, while their husbands walked ahead carrying nothing. After the donkeys arrived, a U.N. worker went to visit to see how the villagers were adapting to having beasts of burden available for the first time. What he discovered, to his horror, was that the husbands were now riding the donkeys while the wives continued to carry the heavy loads!

The point of all this not-so-pleasant information is that there has always been discrimination toward females in recorded history, at least since the beginning of the great civilizations, and it continues today. Today, however, we are living in a period of transition, a time when things are beginning to change (laws, consciousness, religious practices, and so on). But I believe that true equality between the sexes is something that not even your generation will see in its lifetime. So be informed, be prepared, and try to be realistic. Be grateful to the women who came before you and made sacrifices, so that the women who came afterward would be better off. (And believe me, you are better off!) If some of the older women you meet seem angry and anti-male, try to understand and not make judgments, because you do not know their experience. Above all try to demythologize the word *feminist* of all the negative connotations that the sexist media has attached to it so that it is a word (and more) that you can identify with and be proud of.

Love from your feminist father,
Dad

P.S. Lest you think that sexism is an overblown idea, read what two female historians, Carrie Catt and Nettie Shuler, wrote in 1923 about what it took to get the nineteenth amendment passed in 1920, giving women the right to vote:

> To get the word "male" in effect out of the Constitution cost the women of the country fifty-two years of pauseless campaign. . . . During that time they were forced to conduct fifty-six campaigns of referenda to male voters; 480 campaigns to get Legislatures to submit suffrage amendments to voters; 47 campaigns to get State constitutional conventions to write woman suffrage into state constitutions; 277 campaigns to get State party conventions to include woman suffrage planks; 30 campaigns to get presidential party conventions to adopt woman suffrage planks in party platforms, and 19 campaigns with 19 successive congresses.

No small wonder that the women's movement needed some forty years to recover!

Too Steady Too Soon—Relationships

Dear Lili,

You mentioned that you were upset because some girls saw you "hanging out" with a boy other than the one you are dating seriously. You are afraid that your boyfriend will hear about it and become jealous.

First of all, I can't help but wonder whether it is a good idea to get too serious with anyone in your freshman year, even a desirable senior. Now is the time to explore relationships with a lot of different men. I think the tendency to latch on to someone as soon as possible is tempting because it is convenient, and it allays anxiety about our attractiveness. This works against the objective of meeting many members of the opposite sex, which I think is especially important for someone like you who did not date very much in high school and attended a sex-segregated school.

As I tell my statistics class, a direct positive relationship exists between the size of the sample and the quality of the inference. That is, the larger the sample, the better the final conclusion (for example, in mate selection!). So, too, with dating, it seems to me. Better to have some idea of what's available out there before you become a consumer, before you become attached and eventually marry.

I hope you and your boyfriend can reach an understanding that this relationship you have and cherish does not preclude meeting other boys and making new friends. Nothing is worse than being involved with someone who is extremely possessive and causes you to feel guilty every time you even talk to another boy. Possessiveness and jealousy are usually symptoms of insecurity.

I personally feel that another dimension is involved here, and it may sound strange upon first hearing it. I believe that God has a stake in marriage and procreation, and therefore "arranges" for us to meet certain people who would make the most suitable life mates. After reading the book *The Shared Heart,* by Barry and Joyce Vissell, I was convinced of this phenomenon. The Vissells tell of how they met in college and experienced an almost instant realization that they were meant for each other. However, they had one big problem. Barry was Jewish and Joyce was Christian (Lutheran), and they were both very devout in their faith. In fact, when they first met, Joyce assumed that Barry was Christian because they were attending a Lutheran-founded college. Only after she fell in love did she discover that Barry was Jewish. When they discovered the difference in religions, they decided to break off the relationship. But their hearts longed for each other. They realized that they were supposed to get married, and that God would help them resolve their religious differences. Apparently God has, because they are still married after twenty years. They have two beautiful daughters, and they do inspired work in the field of marriage counseling.

So, pray to God to send you the person with whom you are supposed to make your life. In the meantime meet lots of young men: "The larger the sample the better the inference." Make friends, and if you are open to the prompting of the Holy Spirit, you will know in your heart when the right one (soul mate) comes along.

Love,
Dad

Letter to a Student

Dear Lisa, the pseudo-preppy,

So you gave the performance of a lifetime and I missed it! I truly wish I could have been there to see you. I'm sure you were fantastic, and I can't understand why the juniors didn't win the talent show competition. The sophomores must have been quite impressive to take the prize! By the way, it's not the first time that the seniors didn't win. I remember once in the seventies when they didn't win, and again, all hell broke loose. By now everybody has forgotten about it, and there is probably a lesson in that somewhere.

I am so glad you decided to make the retreat next month. I know it will be a wonderful experience for you, as it has been for me. "Hanging out with God" is a pretty powerful trip! Are you familiar with Francis Thompson's poem "The Hound of Heaven"? I recommend you read it before going on the retreat. Dorothy Day, the founder of the Catholic Worker movement and a twentieth-century uncanonized saint, wrote the following about this great poem:

> It is one of those poems that awakens the soul, recalls to it the fact that God is its destiny. The idea of this pursuit fascinated me; the inevitableness of it, the recurrence of it, made me feel that inevitably I would have to pause in the mad rush of living to remember my first beginning and last end.

Be sure to let me know how it goes, and I will pray for you.

I'm also glad to hear that you are getting smart about booze. It really is a dead end that never fulfills its promises. Instead of bringing people closer together, it usually ends up as a barrier to real intimacy—which in its best sense is what we are all thirsting for. I am heartened by the revelation, as reported in the student newspaper, that students are discovering that you don't have to drink in order to have a good time at a party. Those legislators in Albany who raised the minimum age for drinking in New York State are not party poopers after all. In fact, they are lifesavers!

Things are good here on my sabbatical retreat at Saint Mary's Villa in Sloatsburg, New York. I am still able to cross-country ski every day (it's a tough life!), and the sisters (Sister Servants of Mary Immaculate) here are really spoiling me. They are such a delight to live and pray with; I wish you could meet all of them, for they are beautiful, sensitive, intelligent, humble, and holy women. They are teaching me a lot more by example than by words. It reminds me of something that the now-dead Italian-German Jesuit Romano Guardini said about teaching, "It's not so much what we say, nor even what we do, but who we are that speaks the loudest to our students."

With that "pearl of great price," I will take leave of you for now, Dear Heart. Thanks for thinking of me, and as Saint Paul said, *"Esto sobrius!"* Be sober!

Peace and Love,
Dr. Lawry

Finding Your Own Voice

Dear Lili,

I just finished an amazing book that I feel you should know about. It was written by Mary Belenky and several colleagues and is entitled *Women's Ways of Knowing: The Development of the Self, Voice, and Mind.* It's a kind of Piaget-like analysis of how young women develop cognitively in contrast to young men. It identifies seven ways of knowing, or stages of development, that young women seem to go through (or get stuck in). These begin with Silence (characterized by having no voice at all, being filled with self-denial, being completely dependent upon external authority, and frequently having a background of having been abused as children) and end with Constructed Knowledge, an integration of the inner voice (subjective knowledge) and the voice of reason, combined with separate and connected knowing (procedural knowledge). The result is a unique and authentic voice.

One of the arguments of the book is that women in our society (and probably most other people) have difficulty finding their own voice. Language and power are frequently related, and because men have most of the power in our culture, women frequently have difficulty cultivating their own voice. Like children, women should be seen and not heard. (Just as an aside, it was found by Zimmerman and West that 96 percent of cross-sex interruptions in face-to-face conversations were males interrupting females. This in spite of the stereotype of women talking over men in mixed company!)

I told my humanistic psychology class about the book, and they were very excited about its implications. I told them they should make finding their own voice one of their goals before graduation. Shortly after my lecture, a student, Kathleen, was scheduled to give a report on *Love, Medicine and Miracles,* an extraordinary book about the power of love (especially self-love) in the healing of cancer. The author, Bernie Siegel, is a most unusual surgeon who, for example, shaves his head to empathize with his patients' loss of hair due to chemotherapy. Initially Kathleen read from her prepared notes—but all of a sudden she forgot her nervousness and began to talk enthusiastically about her impressions of the book. I reluctantly interrupted her and said to the class: "Did you hear that? Kathleen was just speaking in her own voice!" A silence fell over the room, and finally Kathleen looked up and said, "Now I know what you mean."

May you find your own voice, Sweetheart!

Love,
Dad

"Sadistics"

Dear Lili,

So you are having trouble with statistics, or what the students here-abouts fondly call sadistics. And your father has been teaching the course for more than twenty years! It's too bad that Jean-Baptiste de Lamarck's theory of evolution did not hold up. Lamarck argued for what he called the inheritance of acquired characteristics. If a natural parent develops a skill, then that skill should be inherited by the off-spring. If your father becomes an accomplished statistician, then you should inherit that ability as well. It was an interesting idea, but Charles Darwin had a better idea, namely natural selection, which superseded Lamarck's theory half a century later.

Though I can't give you genes for statistics, I can let you in on a secret that probably applies to a lot of things besides statistics. The way to develop a skill like statistics is to practice it by doing a lot of different kinds of problems. I always assign *all* of the problems at the end of a chapter, because I know that it will better prepare the students for a particular problem on a test, or in real life. The analogy I use in class is an example from tennis. If you want to become great at tennis, play as many different players as possible, as good as if not better than you, so that you learn to adapt to all the different styles of playing. When it comes to a tournament, you will be better prepared for any opponent, regardless of style.

This is how you develop what I call a repertoire. The same thing holds for something like statistics. The more problems you solve before taking the test, the better prepared you will be for the slightly different approach to a solution that every particular problem requires. What is implicit here is what I have written earlier about making mistakes. As you make mistakes in doing the practice problems, you are actually learning not to make them in similar problems. Exposure to a sufficient number and variety of problems on a particular topic, such as the binomial theorem, should help you develop a repertoire for handling most any problem that you encounter on a test, or in life for that matter.

Another principle is operating here as well, Lili, and that is the basic law of practice effect. The more practice you get before a test, the more immune you become to the other variables that can erode performance on a test: unfamiliarity, stress, test anxiety, time pressure, and so on. I call it getting in the groove. In other words, you develop a proficiency that prepares you even for emergency circumstances, such as a "trick" question (which from a teacher's point of view is a good question because it tests whether you can apply what you have learned in a slightly different context).

So, you want to get an A and become a good statistician (God knows there is a tremendous need for them in business). Remember how you get to Carnegie Hall: "Practice! Practice! Practice!" There are no shortcuts, Sweetheart.

Love,
Dad

"The Art of Acknowledgment"

Dear Lili,

I am reading a book by a friend and former colleague, Jean Houston. Jean and I were freshman faculty together in 1965. She left Marymount several years later, but we have remained friends. The name of the book is *The Possible Human: A Course in Extending Your Physical, Mental, and Creative Abilities*. It is vintage Houston, or as Marilyn Ferguson has said, "A master course by a master teacher."

In chapter six, "The Art of High Practice," she distinguishes between the Nebbish, "archetype of the Artist of Low Practice," and the Mensch, "archetype of the Artist of High Practice." In case you are not familiar with these Yiddish terms, Jean describes the attitude of a Nebbish as: "Nobody really wants me. It's just that I'm the only one around." On the other hand, "When a Mensch walks down the street even the sidewalk feels good." Do you get the idea? In other words, there is a Nebbish and a Mensch in all of us, but most of the time we feel like Nebbishes, the Yiddish equivalent of "I'm not OK." But, "we as the Mensch have the power to restore to one another the glory of who we are." Jean calls this power the "art of acknowledgment," appropriately enough.

When Jean was your age, eighteen, a junior in college (having advanced two years), she encountered her first Mensch college professor after a devastating belated sophomore slump. I am going to let her tell her own story as only she can tell it:

> I was eighteen years old and I was the golden girl. A junior in college, I was president of the college drama society, a member of the student senate, winner of two off-Broadway critics' awards for acting and directing, director of the class play, and had just turned down an offer to train for the next Olympics. In class my

mind raced and dazzled, spinning off facile but "wowing" analogies to the kudos of teachers and classmates. Socially, I was on the top of the heap. My advice was sought, my phone rang constantly, and it seemed that nothing could stop me.

I was the envy of all my friends and I was in a state of galloping chutzpah.

The old Greek tragedies warn us that when hubris rises, nemesis falls. I was no exception to this ancient rule. My universe crashed with great suddenness. It began when three members of my immediate family died. Then a friend whom I loved very much died suddenly of a burst appendix while camping alone in the woods. The scenery of the off-Broadway production fell on my head and I was left almost blind for the next four months. My friends and I parted from each other, they out of embarrassment and I because I didn't think I was worthy. My marks went from being rather good to a D-plus average.

I had so lost confidence in my abilities that I couldn't concentrate on anything or see the connections between things. My memory was a shambles, and within a few months I was placed on probation. All my offices were taken away; public elections were called to fill them. I was asked into the advisor's office and told that I would have to leave the college at the end of the spring term since, clearly, I didn't have the "necessary intelligence to do academic work." When I protested that I had had the "necessary intelligence" during my freshman and sophomore years, I was assured with a sympathetic smile that intellectual decline such as this often happened to young women when "they became interested in other things; it's a matter of hormones, my dear."

Where once I had been vocal and high-spirited in the classroom, I now huddled in my oversized camel's-hair coat in the back of classes, trying to be as nonexistent as possible. At lunch I would lock myself in the green room of the college theater, scene of my former triumphs, eating a sandwich in despondent isolation. Every day brought its defeats and disacknowledgments, and after my previous career I was too proud to ask for help. I felt like Job and called out to God, "Where are the boils?" since that was about all I was missing.

These Jobian fulminations led me to take one last course. It was taught by a young Swiss professor of religion, Dr. Jacob Taubes, and was supposed to be a study of selected books of the

Old Testament. It turned out to be largely a discussion of the dialectic between St. Paul and Nietzsche.

Taubes was the most brilliant and exciting teacher I had ever experienced, displaying European academic wizardry such as I had never known. Hegel, gnosticism, structuralism, phenomenology, and the intellectual passions of the Sorbonne cracked the ice of my self-noughting and I began to raise a tentative hand from my huddle in the back of the room and ask an occasional hesitant question. Dr. Taubes would answer with great intensity, and soon I found myself asking more questions.

One day I was making my way across campus to the bus, when I heard Dr. Taubes addressing me: "Miss Houston, let me walk with you. You know, you have a most interesting mind."

"Me? I have a *mind?*"

"Yes, your questions are luminous. Now what do you think *is* the nature of the transvaluation of values in Paul and Nietzsche?"

I felt my mind fall into its usual painful dullness and stammered, "I d-don't know."

"Of course you do!" he insisted. "You couldn't ask the kinds of questions you do without having an unusual grasp of these issues. Now please, once again, what do you think of the transvaluation of values in Paul and Nietzsche? It is important for my reflections that I have your reflections."

"Well," I said, waking up, "if you put it that way, I think . . ."

I was off and running and haven't shut up since.

Dr. Taubes continued to walk me to the bus throughout that term, always challenging me with intellectually vigorous questions. He attended to me. I existed for him in the "realest" of senses, and because I existed for him I began to exist for myself. Within several weeks my eyesight came back, my spirit bloomed, and I became a fairly serious student, whereas before I had been, at best, a bright show-off.

What I acquired from this whole experience was a tragic sense of life, which balanced my previous enthusiasms. I remain deeply grateful for the attention shown me by Dr. Taubes. He acknowledged me when I most needed it. I was empowered in the midst of personal erosion, and my life has been very different for it. I swore to myself then that whenever I came across someone "going under" or in the throes of disacknowledgment, I would try to reach and acknowledge that person as I had been acknowledged.

I would go so far as to say that the greatest of human po-
tentials is the potential of each one of us to empower and acknowledge the other. We all do this throughout our lives, but
rarely do we appreciate the power of the empowering that we
give to others. To be acknowledged by another, especially during
times of confusion, loss, disorientation, disheartenment, is to be
given time and place in the sunshine and is, in the metaphor of
psychological reality, the solar stimulus for transformation.

The process of healing and growth is immensely quickened
when the sun of another's belief is freely given. This gift can be
as simple as "Hot dog! Thou art!" Or it can be as total as "I know
you. You are God in hiding." Or it can be a look that goes
straight to the soul and charges it with meaning.

I have been fortunate to have known several of those the
world deems "saints": Teilhard de Chardin, Mother Teresa of Cal-
cutta, Clemmie, an old black woman in Mississippi. To be looked
at by these people is to be gifted with the look that engenders.
You feel yourself primed at the depths by such seeing. Something
so tremendous and yet so subtle wakes up inside that you are
able to release the defeats and denigrations of years. If I were to
describe it further, I would have to speak of unconditional love
joined to a whimsical regarding of you as the cluttered house that
hides the holy one.

Saints, you say, but the miracle is that anybody can do it for
anybody! Our greatest genius may be the ability to prime the
healing and evolutionary circuits of one another. . . .

It is an art form that has yet to be learned, for it is based on
something never before fully recognized—deep psychological
reciprocity, the art and science of mutual transformation. And all
the gurus and the masters, all the prophets, profs, and profes-
sionals, can do little for us compared to what we could do for
each other if we would but be present to the fullness of each
other. For there is no answer to anyone's anguished cry of "Why
am I here, why am I at all?" except the reply, "Because I am here,
because I am."

May you discover at least one Mensch professor before you graduate, Dear Heart. And may you never forget the "art of acknowledgment" in your dealings with others.

I love you,
Dad

Valentine's Day

Dear Lili,

I just can't get over how the freshmen are responding to Jampolsky's book, *Love Is Letting Go of Fear,* again this semester. The first lesson in the book is, "All that I give is given to myself." Jampolsky shows us that love operates from a principle of abundance, not scarcity. The more we give away, the more we get—just the opposite of what most of us really believe.

I was trying to think of an assignment that would help the students experience the truth of this fundamental lesson. I remembered that Valentine's Day was coming up over the weekend. I asked the students to give a valentine to someone who would not normally expect one from them. I couldn't wait for the weekend to be over. When I asked for volunteers to report on what had happened, at first no one raised a hand. Finally, a tentative hand was raised in the last row. "Dr. Lawry," Michelle began, "I would like to tell the class what happened to me.

"This was a very positive experience; I made a friend. It was February fifteenth, and I was in a long line in the middle of the cold night with a few of my friends. We were waiting to buy tickets to see a rock concert. I was introduced to a guy named Nick. We had all the time in the world because the box office did not open for another five hours, and nothing else was open either. So we talked; everyone else we were with had fallen asleep. By the time the sun came up, we had told each other things about ourselves that we had not even told some of our friends. For example, he told me that his real name was not Nick; he just didn't like his real name and refused to tell anyone otherwise.

"When morning came I remembered the assignment and ran to a store across the street and bought a valentine to give to him. He was

103

surprised and honored. He asked me out to dinner that evening and even told me what his real name is! Since that day we have become good friends.

"We never did get tickets. But later, by chance, he came across two front-row tickets and invited me to go instead of his girlfriend. When I asked him why me, he said because I would appreciate it more, having waited in line so long, and besides he owed me one for the valentine. 'To give is to receive is the law of love.' It sums up the experience exactly."

I was so excited with Michelle's good fortune that I recounted the story to my senior seminar later that day. They had read the Jampolsky book as freshmen, so I knew they would appreciate it. Finally, after recounting the story, one of the seniors asked why I hadn't given *them* the same assignment. Perhaps she would have made a new friend and received an invitation to dinner as well! Suddenly the students all burst into laughter, because they realized that they didn't need an assignment to give a valentine. We always have that option. There is nothing to lose and everything to gain. . . .

Love,
Dad

Growing Up and Saying Good-Bye

Dear Lili,

I just wanted to write and tell you how much I enjoyed your visit last weekend. You were a big hit with all the sisters! They were sincere in inviting you to visit during the summer. We should definitely try to work that in when you come to New York this summer.

You seem to be growing up so quickly now. Each time I see you, it appears that you have grown another year! I have difficulty keeping up with the changes; each visit brings a different person. I can't say I am displeased with the changes. In fact, I feel that you are growing into a very attractive and mature young woman and a good person. It's just that the changes are coming so quickly now as you move from childhood into adulthood.

I hope you will give some serious thought to what I proposed as my preface to the book I am writing. I would like very much that the letters be addressed to you, because that is where the feelings and ideas expressed come from—my relationship with you. I could write to an imaginary student, but somehow that doesn't feel as honest. If perhaps you could share your reservations, then maybe I could understand better. I would hope that the book would make you feel proud of me, wanting to share a few bits of advice accumulated over a career of more than twenty years of college teaching. It doesn't matter if you agree or disagree with the advice. The point is that perhaps other young people like yourself might benefit. The chances of anyone you know personally reading it, I think, are very remote—it's unlikely, after all, to become a best-seller!

In closing I just want to tell you something that I have been meaning to tell you for a long time, and that is how difficult it is for me to say good-bye to you. For some reason it always reminds me of 1974, when I first left you and your mother. I become very sad and awkward. Just wanted you to understand why I didn't wait for the train with you. The dinner time at Saint Mary's Villa was just an excuse. I expect someday that will dissipate, but for now it seems to need more healing. Any thoughts?

Love you,
Dad

Servant Leadership

Dear Lili,

I just discovered a book (another one!) that I am very excited about. It's entitled *Teacher as Servant,* by Robert K. Greenleaf, and it's a fictional parable about a student residence at a large university dedicated to the teaching of servant leadership.

The students who live in the residence are selected from a group of freshmen who have applied, because they responded affirmatively to the question, "Do you want to be a servant?" The book is written through the eyes of a student with the unlikely name of Martin Hedeggar (a play on the name of the famous German existential philosopher Martin Heidegger), who spends four years recording everything that goes on (it seems) in his voluminous journals while living in this unique residence named Jefferson Hall.

The book begins with the following claim:

> For anything new to emerge *there must first be a dream,* an imaginative view of what might be. For something great to happen, there must be a great dream. Then venturesome persons with faith in that dream will persevere to bring it to reality.
>
> Some ideas whose time has come will spread as in a forest fire. But most need the help of a teacher. I had the good fortune to have an extraordinary one. He dreamed a great dream of how servanthood could be nurtured in the young, and he spent his best years in bringing it to pass. I want to tell you about him.

Martin goes on to tell about Professor Billings, housemaster and professor of physics, teacher and servant leader extraordinaire..

The main thesis of the book is that many young people have a natural disposition to be servants in society, but frequently they remain ineffectual because they are naive about power and therefore about leadership as well. What Professor Billings attempts to do is to teach these idealistic youth that servanthood and power are not in-compatible and, indeed, that the best leadership combines both qual-ities.

Though Greenleaf claims he modeled Billings on the character of Leo in Hermann Hesse's novel *Journey to the East,* I can't help but no-tice the strong similarity to Christ. I think it is fairly obvious that Christ taught a great deal about the importance of serving one's fellow women and men. This was dramatized at the Last Supper with the washing of the Apostles' feet. At the same time, Christ showed tremendous ability to lead and shape rather unexceptional men and women into a formidable corps of teachers, preachers, healers, and, eventually, leaders.

The program that you are presently studying in college is osten-sibly preparing you for eventual leadership in the business world. But how much about true leadership are you really learning? And are you learning that the secret of a real leader is to be a servant to all? If not, I want you to read Greenleaf's book, and I practically guarantee that you will have much more insight into the makings of a true leader. I think you can become one.

Love,
Dad

Keeping Holy the Lord's Day

Dear Lili,

I just wanted to tell you how saddened I was to learn that only "one or two girls in the dorm bother to go to Mass on Sunday." I respect your decision not to go, but I am surprised at the fact that so few students seem to be living some sort of spiritual life, at least from external appearances.

You mentioned that religion is almost never discussed either in class or outside of class. I wonder what you talk about in its place. Doesn't anyone question the meaning of life, the purpose of it all? Doesn't anyone worry that the American Dream of career, house in the suburbs, two BMWs in the garage isn't quite going to buy the happiness promised in the commercials on television? Surely *everyone* hasn't bought this myth! I should think that the evidence to the contrary is too overwhelming, beginning with parents, neighbors, soap operas, and public figures. The obvious conclusion is that money isn't going to do it. Nor are drugs, fame, clothes, a beautiful body, and so on.

It is often said that religion is for children and old people. Did you ever wonder about this truism? Perhaps it takes most of a mature life to discover the meaninglessness of the world's riches before one can begin to get beyond them. Maybe you have to get everything before you can discover that it really isn't anything. It's ironic that Christ said we must become like little children again before we can enter the Kingdom of God. Have you ever noticed how much old people resemble children? Perhaps Christ was expressing a basic psychological principle that affects all of us, whether we cooperate or not.

As for religion, keep an open mind. Recognize that you are probably going through a rebellious phase in which you are outgrowing your childish faith before you can begin to transform it into a mature, adult faith. One of the most important thinkers of the twentieth century, Carl Jung, made the following observation in his *Modern Man in Search of a Soul:*

> Among all my patients in the second half of life—that is to say, over thirty-five—there has not been one whose problem in the last resort was not that of finding a religious outlook on life. It is safe to say that every one of them fell ill because he had lost that which the living religions of every age have given to their followers, and none of them has been really healed who did not regain his religious outlook. This of course has nothing whatever to do with a particular creed or membership of a church.

From my point of view, it is very difficult to live in this modern, materialistic world without faith. The "Hound of Heaven" begins to track you down sooner or later. Either you rediscover God or you turn a deaf ear and search frantically for idols that eventually lead to despair.

As I said, keep an open mind, and when life begins to get crazy and make no sense, remember that perhaps it is time to look for God again. Remember, too, that you have been baptized and confirmed in the Holy Spirit, and someday that force, that power, will begin to make itself known. When it does, as Jung says, we can either cooperate or go mad.

What do you think?

Love,
Dad

May You Never Stop Dancing!

Dear Lili,

I was just reading about Richard Bolles's theory of the "three boxes of life": learning, working, and leisure (playing). According to Bolles the life span in this culture is compartmentalized into three boxes in keeping with the following time frame: learning (ages 5–22), working (22–50), and leisure (50–68). Therefore, if Bolles is right, you are in a predominately learning phase, soon to be transformed into a predominately working phase.

Bolles's theory reminded me of Eric Berne's theory of personality known as transactional analysis, or TA. Like Bolles, Berne claims that the personality is composed of three "ego states": "parent" (your superego, your conscience, your sense of right and wrong), "adult" (your logical-efficient self, the computer), and "child" (your playful, creative, rebellious, smart-aleck self). These ego states are usually represented by three contiguous circles (see diagram A). According to Berne, one of the great hazards of the twentieth century is "atrophication," or the shrinking of the child in us as we proceed into and through adulthood. (This is represented in diagram B.) In other words, we have a tendency to neglect the child within all of us, especially the capacity to play.

These theories challenge us to maintain harmony and wholeness. How can we be a student while at the same time develop good working habits *and* playing habits? If you are able to reach some harmony and integration of these three boxes while you are a college student, then you are not likely to allow the atrophication of your precious child.

Unfortunately, as we grow older, we tend to lose our playfulness. Certainly the culture does not encourage it. Frequently the admonitions to "grow up" and "act your age" are insidious injunctions against

111

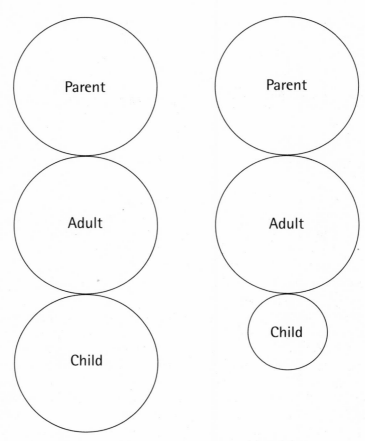

Diagram A.
The three ego states of
Transactional Analysis showing
healthy proportionate size.

Diagram B.
The three ego states of
Transactional Analysis showing
"atrophication" of the child
ego state.

being a child. Often implicit in these remarks is a kind of ageism, or discrimination against the elderly (anyone over thirty for your generation!). I remember Ashley Montagu writing in *Psychology Today* several years ago about his experience of going to dances as a senior citizen with his wife and incurring the stares and remarks of the young people who obviously felt they didn't belong there. The young people perceived the old couple as pathetic examples of old men and women trying to recapture their youth rather than seeing them as vital senior citizens who still knew how to play and have fun. They are personalities for whom the child is still a dynamic dimension.

So, Dear Heart, study hard and work hard, but don't ever lose your wonderful capacity to play and have fun. The temptation will be strong to be "grown up" when you graduate and take on the full responsibilities of adulthood. I see the recent graduates who return to visit so transformed in their manner and dress, so grown up. But I worry that the child within is starving. Remember that Jesus taught that we must become like "little children" in order to enter the Kingdom of God (Matthew 18:3). I think that Christ, the great psychologist that he was, is simply reminding us of a great and profound truth: if we fail to love the child within, we risk losing the capacity to *wonder* and to see God.

May you never stop dancing!

Love,
Dad

The Classics: An Opinion

Dear Lili,

This is a follow-up to my letter on "Falling in Love with the Library." What I would like to do is share with you some of my reading journal that I kept while an undergraduate. Yes, I actually kept a journal in which I listed and commented on every book I read between 1959 and 1962 while studying for the priesthood. The best part of keeping such a journal is being able to go back at my age and read what I wrote when I was your age. I hope you will consider doing the same.

Unlike yourself, I was a virtual nonreader until I began college. True, I was a voracious comic book reader as a child, and that is probably how I learned to read. However, I never matured beyond that as a reader until college. I am embarrassed to admit that I don't think I read one book, cover to cover, throughout four years of high school. I remember trying to read *Jane Eyre,* by Charlotte Brontë, but could not get beyond the first three hundred pages. I know I was intimidated by the sheer length of it, but I also realize now that I really did not understand what Brontë was trying to say about love and passion.

A number of things happened to me in college that converted me into a reader, but I will share just two. The first was meeting a young college graduate who had received a very meager and inadequate secondary education and whose reading background was especially deficient. He told me that he never realized his shortcomings until his freshman year in a very competitive college. Listening to his fellow students discuss, defend, and criticize the books they were reading in an English literature class, he quickly became aware of his inferior knowledge of the world's greatest literature. He decided to remedy the situation, and the following summer saw him digest thirty of the Great Books that Mortimer Adler lists in *How to Read a Book.*

I was very impressed with his motivation and felt challenged to do the same.

The second important experience I had was the serendipitous discovery of the aforementioned *How to Read a Book* while browsing in the college library one evening. In some ways Adler's book opened up a whole new world for me. For one thing, it taught me how to read for understanding as well as for information. Adler defines reading as "the process whereby a mind, with nothing to operate on but the symbols of the readable matter, and with no help from outside, elevates itself by the power of its own operations." In other words the reader must be active not passive, should ask questions, and, in effect, should dialog with the author as if he or she were actually present.

The other thing that Adler's book did for me was to introduce me to what are called, for lack of a better name, the classics. Adler lists six criteria that a book must have to be worthy of the title "classic." They must be:

- the most widely read (down through the centuries)
- popular and not pedantic
- always contemporary
- the most readable
- the most instructive and enlightening
- engaged with the persistently involved problems of human life

For me, the salient characteristic of a classic is its originality. With its inception, a new and provocative idea is injected into the mainstream of thought, or at least a venerable and universal truth is arrayed with such freshness and youthful attire that it takes on new meaning. It is in this feature of the classics that we find their essential significance. They are the bridges that we must cross in order to reach the "world of ideas." As Thoreau put it so well, "Read not the Times. Read the Eternities."

Not only does Adler teach you how to read the classics but he also includes a list of what have come to be known as the Great Books. And so I was off and running with the *Dialogues* of Plato, the *Iliad* and the *Odyssey* of Homer, and the plays of Aeschylus, Euripides, and Sophocles. (My favorites were *Medea,* by Euripides, and *Antigone,* by Sophocles. I liked *Medea* because it dramatizes the close connection between love and hate, and I liked *Antigone* because it is a story of family honor and loyalty.) *The Histories* of Herodotus and

The History of the Peloponnesian War, by Thucydides, brought history to life for me in a way that none of my history courses ever did.

From the Greeks I jumped into the nineteenth century with Thomas Hardy's *Tess of the D'Urbervilles* and *The Return of the Native.* (I don't think I ever told you that I wanted to name you Eustacia after the exotic character in *The Return of the Native,* but your mother wouldn't hear of it!) I also discovered Tennyson's *Idylls of the King,* and that got me hooked on poetry. I loved reading about the great romances of King Arthur and Lancelot and Guinevere, and I carried that little book with me everywhere.

Moving into the twentieth century, I would say that the most formative authors for me were Graham Greene, Evelyn Waugh, and J. D. Salinger. Greene taught me compassionate understanding for the "sinners" of the world, such as the whiskey priest in *The Power and the Glory* and the adulterous woman in *The End of the Affair.* Waugh taught me about sophistication and satire in *Brideshead Revisited.* Finally, Salinger validated my adolescent angst in *The Catcher in the Rye* and my spiritual longing in *Franny and Zooey.*

I also have to mention Betty Smith's *A Tree Grows in Brooklyn.* The portrayal of Francie Nolan's courage to survive against all odds made an impression on me at the time that I shall never forget. I am sure I would find it sentimental today, but back then it was a compass and an inspiration on the road through adolescence.

Well, Sweetheart, I hope that gives you some idea of the kind of reading that I did while in college and how it helped me to grow and mature. I believe that creating a bibliography (and library!) of important books can be a treasured part of your life's journey. (It saddens me when I ask my freshmen classes to name an important book in their life and many cannot name one!) I hope therefore that you are inspired to create your own bibliography. Good reading!

Love,
Dad

Just Friends

Dear Lili,

I just finished attending an alumnae reunion at Marymount and was struck by the fact that so many former students have remained good friends since graduation from college. It would seem that a bonding process goes on during one's adolescence, and that is why we keep so many friends from high school and college. In the case of college graduates, I think, there is a greater tendency to keep friends from college than from high school. There are obvious exceptions, of course, and indeed one of my best friends is a friend from high school who was the best man in my wedding.

I also wonder whether the friends that women make at a women's college like Marymount differ in kind from the friends that women make at coed colleges. My sense is that more competition exists among women at coed colleges. The women's movement may have changed that to some degree, but I can't help but wonder whether some differences remain! Could this be one of the reasons women's colleges in the United States produce proportionately more high-achieving women than do their coed counterparts? Is the women's college environment more supportive of women students for this reason as well as for all the other reasons that have been researched (like more female role models and teachers who take their female students more seriously)? It is an interesting question that I hope someone will research someday.

My definition of a friend is someone who always tells me the truth, even though I may not wish to hear it. Of course that works both ways. A friend is also someone I can confide in and who will listen without judgment, or as the American philosopher George Santayana put it, one's friends "are that part of the race with which one can be human." This bond is so close that Aristotle, the great Greek philosopher, described friendship as "a single soul dwelling in two bodies." Friendship for him was so important that "without friends no one would choose to live, though he had all other goods." A pretty strong statement! Indeed, I think our friends are like mirrors to ourselves. If you want to see yourself, look carefully at your friends. That certainly has been true in my case as I think of the many different friends I have made over the years.

Teaching at a women's college, I am often made aware of the difference between female friendship and male friendship. It is only recently that Hollywood has begun to get over its love affair with male buddies such as Butch Cassidy and the Sundance Kid. In recent years we have been treated to movies about female friends such as Thelma and Louise, and the circles of women in *How to Make an American Quilt* and *The Spitfire Grill*. Columnist Ellen Goodman points out that such a change in focus reflects "a shift, not just from men to women but from one definition of friendship to another."

One of the differences that I notice is how much more physical college-aged female friends are with one another than males are. There is a lot more hand holding, touching, hugging, sitting close to each other in the dining room, and so on. Males seem to keep greater distance. I suppose we males are still suffering from homophobia, fear of homosexuality. The only kinds of touching that seem to be okay with adolescent males are hitting and sports-related congratulatory gestures.

I remember a student who wrote that her best friend had just been tested for cancer. When she went into her friend's room to find out what the results of the biopsy were, she found her in bed crying. She wrote that the only thing she could think of doing was to climb into bed and hold her friend and cry with her. She knew that no words would be adequate to the sadness. This anecdote captures the essence of what is peculiarly female in friendship. No male that I know could imagine doing this with his best male friend. For one thing, men learn very early that big boys don't cry, and if they do cry, it had better be in private.

I think one of the fringe benefits of the women's movement is that it is redefining the meaning of friendship. I am impressed by the prescience of the English poet Samuel Taylor Coleridge in this insight expressed over one hundred fifty years ago: "A woman's friendship borders more closely on love than man's. Men affect each other in the reflection of noble or friendly acts, whilst women ask fewer proofs and more signs and expressions of attachment." First came consciousness-raising groups, and now we have women's support groups. Only more recently have men begun to see the advantage of forming a group of males for mutual support and bonding. I think men have begun to question the folk wisdom reflected in a remark attributed to President Harry Truman, "You want a friend for life, get a dog."

Well, Lili, you might be wondering why this sermon on friends and friendships. It may seem almost to border on the obvious. Of course your friends mean a lot to you. But I think it's important to reflect on just how significant our friends are in our life. I suspect that we tend to take them for granted. We probably should choose friends as carefully as we choose lovers, but I believe we usually choose friends because they are people who are most like us and therefore the most comfortable. That may not always be the best criterion for selection. Writing about soul mates, Barry and Joyce Vissell, in their book *The Shared Heart,* say something like, the mind chooses an easy partner but the heart chooses someone who will help us to grow. I think that should be true for friends as well.

In closing I would like to quote from Lillian Rubin's book *Just Friends,* in which she reminds us:

> We need our friends—not just for fun, not just for a replacement for a distant or difficult family or a failed marriage, not just because they can provide the human framework within which we can make good the deficits of the past. All are crucial to our well-being. But we need our friends also because they serve developmental imperatives at every stage of life, because the turning points and transitions that are the inevitable accompaniments of living would be infinitely harder to negotiate without them.

May you have many good friends in your lifetime!

Love,
Dad

Surfing the Web

Dear Lili,

What can I say about the World Wide Web? I'm a book person! After talking with you last night, I realize that we have very different perspectives about the Web and the Internet. You see it as just one more source of information in the evolving spiral of cyberspace. I see it as a major paradigm shift in the way we think and communicate with one another. You grew up with computers, and I grew up with the typewriter!

I must confess that I am ambivalent about the Internet. On the one hand, you are right, it is an extraordinary resource and potential educational tool. It is like having a major library at your fingertips. And although you must be much more discriminating about the quality (veracity even) of what you find, it is an incredible time-saver and potential gold mine of information.

The downside is that it puts us at greater distance from one another. At the same time it improves communication and the opportunity for meeting more people, it obviates the face-to-face encounter that we now know is so crucial to human development in infants, and also in everyone else. A number of my students have "met" boyfriends on the Internet that they might not have met otherwise. But I get the impression that when reality intervenes (that is, when they get to know each other in person), the relationship is in jeopardy. I suppose it is easy to fall in love with someone's poetry, but a relationship involves a lot more than beautiful words on a computer screen.

I also suspect that the Internet has a potential addictive quality, especially for the introverted and shy among us. It is much less threatening to engage people online than in person. Also, there is some weird and apparently seductive stuff out there. I just read a piece called "kook.com" in *Time Digital* that describes a twenty-four-year-old young woman who broadcasts live pictures—updated every minute—of the space under her bed, where she suspects that monsters live. "My goal is to get the rest of the connected world to help me understand what the hell is happening in my house," she says. "Kind of a virtual neighborhood watch."

What can you say about that except that, if nothing else, it confirms just how prophetic Marshall McLuhan was in his vision of the global village. A "virtual neighborhood watch" of the space under someone's bed!

Well, Dear Heart, I'm sure that this will sound very quaint if not antediluvian in a few years, but there it is. Just be discriminating, and remember that virtual reality is never a substitute for reality.

Love,
Dad

A Citizen of the World

Dear Lili,

I was talking to a senior who had just returned from a year of studying in England, and I was impressed by how much more mature she seemed than when she left. Granted she is a year older, but I don't think anything compares to studying a year (or even a semester or a summer) abroad to contribute to one's education in the best sense of the word.

I was reminded of your senior year of high school, when you were an exchange student in Sweden. I think it will be years before you fully appreciate how that experience has contributed to your education, not to mention your maturation. To learn a new language, to live with a new family, to go to a new school, to live in a new climate (southern Lapland)—what a wonderful opportunity to transcend the "culture trance," as the anthropologists call it. Growing up exclusively in one culture or one country, we begin to assume the whole world thinks and behaves the way we and our neighbors do.

I remember your comment that Swedish high school students seemed to be much more serious about their studies in general than American students, and especially about politics and affairs of the world. They seemed to be much more knowledgeable and curious about America than we are about Sweden and the world in general. I suppose that is what people label the arrogance of Americans, their belief that the United States is the center of the world. It is good to learn that the United States does not have a monopoly on "life, liberty, and the pursuit of happiness," as our Constitution puts it. In fact, I think we could learn a lot from the Swedes in the area of health care and social welfare, to name just two examples.

I will never forget my visit to Sweden during spring break that year and how proud I was of you in your fluency with the Swedish language after only seven months and not knowing even a word of Swedish when you began your adventure. I was also proud of your recently acquired knowledge of the country, its people, and its history. If I believed in reincarnation, I would have to conclude that you must have been a Swede in a previous lifetime; you took to the country like a duck to water, as they say. You even look Swedish with your high cheekbones and golden hair.

What that experience must have done for your confidence! To think that at the age of seventeen you left your family to live and go to school in a foreign country with strangers whose language you did not even speak. I am not sure I had that kind of confidence when I was your age. And what wonderful adventures you had: your first real boyfriend, an opportunity to live with a "sister," going to dances and basketball games, skiing in the mountains and shopping in the stores, and visiting other countries like Denmark, France, Finland, Germany, and the Soviet Union, speaking Swedish so fluently that some Europeans mistook you for a Swede.

Well, Sweetheart, I hope this will not be the end of your travels abroad. They have too much to teach you to neglect them. Perhaps someday you will have the opportunity to go to Southeast Asia as I did in the late seventies. There you will find cultures and traditions entirely different from the so-called Eurocentric one that you are now more familiar with. The world is shrinking into what Marshall McLuhan, the late Canadian philosopher of the media, labeled the global village. If you want to go into business, and I know you do, then you must begin to develop a global perspective. Indeed, it is the ecological movement that is teaching us that "we are all rowing the same boat," as someone put it recently. That is both frightening and challenging. The only way we can begin to start rowing in the same direction is to learn about and understand one another better. How better to do that than to study abroad!

May you truly become a citizen of the world!

Love,
Dad

To the Seniors

Dear Seniors,

Although I am on sabbatical, I want to say good-bye before you leave. I also want to share a few thoughts with you before you take off from this modern-day launching pad into the vale of full adult responsibility.

First of all, I want to tell you how moved I was to learn of your generosity and success in raising funds for multiple sclerosis. As you may not know, my father was stricken with MS when in his thirties, and he has been an invalid ever since. I have seen firsthand how terrible this disease is, not only for the individual but for each member of the immediate family as well. I am grateful to all of you for contributing to the treatment and, hopefully, the cure of people like my father.

Second, I want to recommend that you consider what I am doing before you get enmeshed in your career, and that is to make a retreat. As some of you know, I am making a three-month retreat as part of my sabbatical. I am not recommending three months, but a short retreat would be a graduation gift (to yourself) that you will value for the rest of your life. Spending a few days in silence, with assistance from a good spiritual director, will create a space for you in which to ask the kinds of questions that you may not even know you have until the noise dies down. I speak of questions such as these: "Now that I am graduated, what is my next step?" "Do I really want to spend the rest of my life doing this kind of work?" "What can I do to repay the universe for giving me opportunities that 99 percent of the world just dreams about?" And perhaps most important, "What does God want me to do with my life, and why was I put here in the first place?"

If you need help locating a retreat center, I know that the campus minister would love to assist you.

Finally, I want to congratulate you on your achievements over the past four years, both those that can be seen and recorded and those only you (and God) know about. I hope the college has lived up to your expectations and that you will be proud to be counted among its alumnae. Before you leave, thank the people who deserve your gratitude (chances are that you will never see them again), and forgive those with whom you still have a grievance (for the same reason). I know I speak for all the faculty when I tell you we love you and are proud of you, though it is sometimes difficult for us to express it. And whatever you do, be yourself . . . your best self.

God bless you,
Dr. Lawry

The First Year's the Hardest

Dear Lili,

I can't believe the year is almost over. In a few short weeks you will no longer be a freshman but a veteran sophomore. During the remaining three years, it will never be the same as your freshman year. As you yourself said on the phone the other night with a tinge of anxiety, "Dad, I won't be one of the 'new girls' on campus next year." Yes, by now you have learned the ropes, and you are a familiar face on campus. You have become a bona fide member of the student community. You have "paid your dues." Thank God that doesn't include hazing anymore. (In case you are not familiar with the term, *hazing* refers to a practice that was popular in the fifties and early sixties that Webster's dictionary defines as, "to harass with abusive or ridiculous tricks, usually directed toward freshmen as a kind of initiation rite." It has been largely stamped out because of its tendency toward violent and inflammatory behavior and speech.)

Though you may not feel it, you have grown up quite a bit during this academic year. I know this growth has not always been easy. But the scars should disappear with time. You haven't made straight A's, but your grades are more than respectable. You definitely belong where you are, in a so-called competitive school. You have shown that you can compete with your classmates and that the admissions office did not make a mistake when it accepted your application.

You may not believe it, Sweetheart, but you have just finished the most difficult year of college. I repeat what I said to you on the phone the other night. I am very proud of you.

Love,
Dad

Acknowledgments *(continued)*

The scriptural quotations in this book are from the New Jerusalem Bible. Copyright © 1985 by Darton Longman and Todd, London, and Doubleday, a division of Bantam Doubleday Dell Publishing Group, New York.

The excerpt on page 29 by Jean-Jacques Servan-Schreiber is from *Time,* 16 June 1986, page 53.

The excerpt on pages 30–32 is from *Exploring the Inner World: A Guidebook for Personal Growth and Renewal,* by Tolbert McCarroll (New York: New American Library, 1976), pages 6–15. Copyright © 1974 by Tolbert McCarroll. Reprinted by permission of Julian Press, a division of Crown Publishers.

The excerpt on page 45 by Hippocrates is quoted from *The Hippocrates Diet and Health Program,* by Ann Wigmore (Wayne, NJ: Avery Publishing Group, 1984), page 9. Copyright © 1984 by Ann Wigmore and the Hippocrates Health Institute.

The excerpt on page 50 is from *The Path to No-Self,* by Bernadette Roberts (Boston: Shambhala, 1985), page 153. Copyright © 1985 by Bernadette Roberts.

The first excerpt on page 51 is from *Love Is Letting Go of Fear,* by Gerald G. Jampolsky, MD (New York: Bantam Books, 1981), page 65. Copyright © 1970 by Gerald G. Jampolsky and Jack O. Keeler.

The second excerpt on page 51 is from *A Course in Miracles* (Tiburon, CA: Foundation for Inner Peace, 1975), page 522. Copyright © 1975 by the Foundation for Inner Peace.

The excerpt on page 60 by Robert Eliot is from "Stress: Can We Cope?" in *Time,* 6 June 1983, page 48.

The excerpts on pages 68 by F. Scott Fitzgerald are from *The Letters of F. Scott Fitzgerald,* edited by Andrew Turnbull (New York: Charles Scribner's Sons, 1963), pages 15–16, 28, and 96. Copyright © 1963 by Frances Scott Fitzgerald Lanahan.

The excerpt on page 68 by Charlie W. Shedd is from *Letters to Karen: On Keeping Love in Marriage* (New York: Avon Books, 1968), page 13. Copyright © 1965 by Abingdon Press.

The Census Bureau statistics on page 79 are from *U.S. News and World Report,* 25 November 1985, page 56.

The excerpt from the Bureau of Labor Statistics report on page 79 is from *U.S. News and World Report,* 16 September 1996, page 92.

The excerpt on page 80 by Alexander Pope is taken from *The Oxford Dictionary of Quotations,* 4th ed., edited by Angela Partington (Oxford: Oxford University Press, 1992), page 521. Selection and arrangement copyright © 1979, 1992 by Oxford University Press.

The ideas attributed to Abloff and Hewitt on page 86 are from "Attraction to Men and Women Varying in Self-Esteem," by Richard Abloff and Jay Hewitt, in *Psychological Reports,* volume 56, 1985, pages 615–618. Copyright © 1985 by Psychological Reports.

The research of Winchel, Fenner, and Shaver referred to on page 87 is from "Impact of Coeducation on 'Fear of Success' Imagery Expressed by Male and Female High School Students," by Ronald Winchel, Diane Fenner, and Phillip Shaver, in *Journal of Educational Psychology,* volume 66, number 5, 1974, pages 726–730.

The male-female wage ratios related on page 88 are from "Male/Female Careers—The First Decade: A Study of MBAs," by Mary Anne Devanna, PhD (New York: Columbia University Graduate School of Business, 1984), page 26. Copyright © 1984 by the Columbia University Graduate School of Business.

The excerpt on page 90 is from *Woman Suffrage and Politics,* by Carrie Chapman Catt and Nettie Rogers Shuler (New York: Charles Scribner's Sons, 1923), page 107, as quoted in *Century of Struggle: The Woman's Rights Movement in the United States,* by Eleanor Flexner (New York: Atheneum, 1974), page 173. Copyright © 1959, 1968, 1972 by Eleanor Flexner.

The excerpt on page 93 is from *Meditations: Dorothy Day,* selected and arranged by Stanley Vishnewski (New York: Paulist Press, 1970), page 9. Copyright © 1970 by The Missionary Society of St. Paul the Apostle in the State of New York.

The excerpt on pages 99–102 by Jean Houston is from *The Possible Human: A Course in Extending Your Physical, Mental, and Creative Abilities* (Los Angeles: J. P. Tarcher, 1982), pages 121–127. Copyright © 1982 by Jean Houston. Used by permission of the Putnam Publishing Group.

The excerpt on page 107 is from *Teacher as Servant: A Parable,* by Robert K. Greenleaf (New York: Paulist Press, 1979), pages 9–10. Copyright © 1979 by Robert K. Greenleaf.

The excerpt on page 110 by Carl Jung is from *Modern Man in Search of a Soul,* translated by W. S. Dell and Cary F. Baynes (New York: Harcourt, Brace and World, Harvest Book, 1933), page 229.

The excerpt on page 115 by Mortimer Adler is from *How to Read a Book,* revised and updated edition, by Mortimer J. Adler and Charles Van Doren (New York: Simon and Schuster, 1972), page 8. Copyright © 1972 by Mortimer J. Adler and Charles Van Doren.

The excerpts on pages 117, 118, and 118–119, by George Santayana, Ellen Goodman, and Samuel Taylor Coleridge are from *Close to Home,* by Ellen Goodman (New York: Simon and Schuster, 1979), pages 141, 140, and 140, respectively. Copyright © 1979 by the Washington Post Company.

Notes

Notes

Notes

Notes

Notes

Notes

Praise for the original edition:

"Lawry has ably identified critical life issues for his daughter's success as a college undergraduate. . . . He has written about lessons that took him a long time to learn." *Newsletter of the Jesuit Association of Student Personnel Administrators*

"In a sensible and affectionate style, Lawry offers advice on practical topics. . . . Good reading matter for a college freshman just starting out or a high school senior getting ready for the big change in September." *Catholic New York*

"A heartwarming and thoughtful work that explores the many facets of adapting to life and the college experience." *Duquesne University Record,* Pittsburgh, PA